INDEX VERBORUM

OF THE

FRAGMENTS OF THE AVESTA

COLUMBIA UNIVERSITY

INDO-IRANIAN SERIES

EDITED BY

A. V. WILLIAMS JACKSON

PROFESSOR OF INDO-IRANIAN LANGUAGES
IN COLUMBIA UNIVERSITY

Volume IV

INDEX VERBORUM

OF THE

FRAGMENTS OF THE AVESTA.

BY

MONTGOMERY SCHUYLER, Jr., M.A.,

SOMETIME FELLOW IN INDO-IRANIAN LANGUAGES
IN COLUMBIA UNIVERSITY

AMS PRESS INC.
NEW YORK
1965

Reprinted with Permission of the

Original Publisher, 1965

AMS PRESS INC.

New York, N. Y. 10003

Manufactured in the United States of America

PREFACE.

My desire in compiling this Index has been to render easily accessible a large body of lexicographical material hitherto almost neglected by scholars. A few scattered studies of the fragments of the Avesta have been made and a number of the extant texts have been collected and provisionally translated by Darmesteter in the third volume of his *Zend Avesta* (Paris, 1893). But the study of the vocabulary of the fragments has received very little attention and the reason for this is not difficult of explanation. For the study of the Avesta proper, scholars have long had the advantage of possessing Justi's admirable *Handbuch der Zend-sprache*. But for the fragments there has been no such help. In the present volume, therefore, I have taken the first steps toward such a lexicon by collecting as far as possible each occurrence of every form of all words used in the fragments. I have not made in any sense a dictionary, for that is an impossible task until more exhaustive studies of the fragments shall have been made; but I have given the forms as found in the texts comprising the extant portions of the Avestan nasks not included in Geldner's great edition of the Avesta. These forms will give the necessary data as to the fragments in the Avestan dictionary which Professors Geldner and Jackson are to make. Many new words and new forms have come to light during the progress of the work but all study of such new material must be reserved for some later occasion.

Many problems have arisen during the preparation of this Index. Several of these may be noted here for convenience. First, in collecting the widely scattered material it has sometimes happened that words or phrases have been found apparently in their original Avestan form which really have been retranscribed

from the Pahlavi versions.   Such, for example, are some of the
formulas found in West's Pahlavi treatises in the Sacred Books
of the East, especially in the Dīnkart.   Some words will be found
in this Index which are, perhaps, rather Pāzand than true Avestan
forms.   It has seemed better to include rather than to omit them.
Again in the case of compound words usually written as single
words in the manuscripts, my rule has been to leave unseparated
all verbs used with prepositions but to separate by a hyphen each
compound word properly so-called.   Thus we have *hąmpaθyeiti*
but *hąm-parštəm*.   Cross references have been given in all cases
where any difficulty in finding the compound form might reason-
ably be expected.   This although entirely out of the province of an
Index verborum will, it is hoped, be found of material assistance.

There are other fragments of the Avesta which are not included
in this volume.   For the omission of these no apology is necessary.   Hidden as they are in unknown manuscripts, lost in the
recesses of libraries in India and Persia, they are not accessible
to scholars.   Every little while some new fragment is discovered.
After this volume had gone to the press, Professor Jackson re-
turned from India with some fragments which Professor Geldner
and he intend to edit and translate in the near future.   The col-
lection and editing of these texts is a task of the first importance.
The late Professor Darmesteter while in Bombay, pointed out the
great value which accurate reproductions of these texts would have.
The first fruits of his suggestions may be seen in the zincographic
reproduction of the Pahlavi treatise *Nīrangistān* (ed. D.D. P. Sanjana, Bombay, 1894) the use of which in the preparation of this
Index has corrected many faulty readings in the published texts
of the work and yielded a number of interesting variants.

It gives me great pleasure to thank The New Era Printing
Company for their care in the preparation of this volume.   More
than a little praise is due the compositors and proof-readers who,
in the face of an entirely new and strange subject-matter and a
not too legible chirography, have "followed copy" with such
absolute fidelity and accuracy that it has been almost impossible
to detect any mistakes in their work.   Whatever errors may be

found in the text must be ascribed to the compiler who alone is responsible.

To the kindness of Dr. E. W. West I am indebted for the use of his copy of the rare edition of the *Vijirkart-i Dīnīk*, and to Dr. Louis H. Gray, my friend and fellow-student, I owe many helpful suggestions.

I cannot close this preface and thus finish my labor on the present volume without expressing my debt of gratitude to my friend and teacher, Professor A. V. Williams Jackson. Without his encouragement and constant ready help in all questions both of conception and execution I should often have been tempted to abandon the dreary and mechanical task of compiling and of preparing this Index for the press. His wide knowledge of all matters pertaining to Avestan philology and his kindly criticism have been constantly at my disposal and to his care whatever value this work may have is due.

MONTGOMERY SCHUYLER, JR.

COLUMBIA UNIVERSITY
    IN THE CITY OF NEW YORK,
        November 1st, 1901.

ABBREVIATIONS.

A.   *Aogəmadaēča.* Ed. Geiger, Erlangen, 1878. Also in LeZA., iii., 154–166 = SBE., iv²., 372–386.

AG.   *Afrīn Gāhānbār* in LeZA., iii., 180–187.

APZ.   *Afrīn Paigāmbar Zartušt* = Yt. **23.** of Westergaard.

Bd.   *Būndahišn* in SBE., v., 1–151.

BkN.   *Bakān Yašt Nask* in SBE., xxxvii., 471.

CB.   *Ciθrəm buyāṯ* in Sachau, Neue Beitr., Wien, 1871 = Sitzb. d. kais. Ak. Phil-hist-Cl. Also in LeZA., iii., 148 (FD. 1.) = SBE., iv²., 369.

D.   *Darmesteter, Le Zend Avesta,* iii., Paris, 1893 = Musée Guimet, vol. xxiv.

Dāṯ.   *Dāṯistān-ī Dīnīk* in SBE., xviii., 1–276.

Dk.   *Dīnkarṯ* in SBE., xxxvii. and xlvii. (P. Sj.), added to Dk., refers to the edition of Peshotan Sanjana, and is quoted by volume and page.

Ep. M.   *Epistles of Manūščīhar* in SBE., xviii., 277–366.

F. D.   *Fragments Divers* in LeZA., iii., 149–153 = SBE., iv²., 369–371. FD. 1 = CB; FD. 2 = HtN., p. 485; FD. 3 = HtN., 483; FD. 6 = HtN., p. 485, and SlS. **13.** 6.

Ganj.   *Ganješāyagān.* Ed. P. Sanjana, Bombay, 1885. Quoted by sections.

HtN.   *Hāṯōxt Nask* in SBE., xlvii., 483–487.

LeZA.   *Darmesteter, Le Zend Avesta,* i.–iii., Paris, 1892–93.

Mād-ch.   *Mādīgāne Chatrang.* (*Māṯīgān-ī čatrang.*) Ed. P. Sanjana, Bombay, 1885. Quoted by sections.

Māh Yt.   In *Darmesteter, Études iraniennes,* ii., 292–294. Paris, 1883.

N.   *Nīrangistān* in LeZA., iii., 78–148.

Pars. *Parsenhandschrift* in Trans. du 3me Cong. des Orientalistes, ii., 493–592. St. Petersburg, 1879.

PI. *Patet īrānī* in LeZA., iii., 167–180.

Phl. Vd. *Pahlavi Vendīdād.* Ed. Spiegel, Wien, 1853.

Phl. Ys. *Pahlavi Yasna.* Ed. Spiegel, Wien, 1858.

SBE. *Sacred Books of the East.* Ed. F. Max Müller.

SkN *Sakāṭūm Nask* in SBE., xlvii., 480.

SlS. *Shāyast la-Shāyast* in SBE., v., 237–406.

T. *Tahmuras' Fragments* in LeZA., iii., 53–77 = SBE., iv²., 275–299.

Vij. *Vijirkarṭ-ī Dīnīk.* Ed. Peshotan, Bombay, 1848.

VS. Extr. *Vendīdād Sade.* Fragmentary extracts in Westergaard, p. 485.

Vth. *Vaēθa Fragment* in Journal Asiatique,1886, ii.,182–186.

Vtp. *Vištāsp Yašt* (**24.**) in Westergaard, Zendavesta.

W. *Fragments* published in Westergaard, pp. 331–334.

W. Yt. **21.**

Yt. **22.** In Westergaard, Zendavesta. Copenhagen,

Yt. (APZ.) **23.** 1852–54.

Yt. (Vtp.) **24.**

ZPGl. *Zand-Pahlavi Glossary.* Ed. Haug, Bombay, 1867. (R.) indicates the edition of Dr. Hanns Reichelt, Frahang i oīm. In WZKM. xiv., 177–213 ; xv., 119–196.

Zsp. *Zāṭ-sparam* in SBE. v., 153–187 and xlvii., 131 170.

INDEX VERBORUM

a.

aiᵧsritīm N. 10. cf. *aini°*.

aiθivatəm Yt. 22. 35.

aiθivantəm A. 28.

aiθisritīm N. 10. v. 1. *aiθsritim*.

aiθyejaṇh cf. *iθ°*.

aiθyejaṇhuntəm Yt. 22. 16, 34 ; Yt. (Vtp.) 24. 62.

aiθra T. 47 (read *iθra*.).

aiθra-paititim N. 11. cf. *aēθ°*.

aiδim Yt. 22. 13.

aipi N. 67, 95.

aipi-jasaiti Yt (APZ) 23. 8.

aipi-vərəčainti N. 95.

aiwi N. 81, 84 ; Phl. Vd. 5. 34 ; Vij. p. 89.

aiwiərətō N. 103.

aiwi-garəδmahe N. 20.

aiwigāmi N. 46, 47, 50, 51, 103.

aiwigāme SkN. p. 480 ; ZPGl. 38. 6.

aiwiᵧnixta Phl. Vd. 5. 34 (2) ; Vij. p. 87.

aiwičičišmnāi N. 63.

aiwitəm Yt. 22. 17, 35 ; Yt. (Vtp.) 24. 63.

aiwiθwərəs N. 62.

aiwi-vaiδayeiti N. 81.

aiwi-vaxšayaṭ N. 73. v. l. *aiwa°*.

aĩwi-vinaṭ Yt. (Vtp.) 24. 10.

aiwisurunvaiti N. 26, 60.

aiwisrunāiti N. 24.

aiwisrunvaiti N. 26.

aiwi-srunvanti N. 60.

aiwisrūθrəm ZPGl. 42. 9.

aiwisrūθrəmananąm N. 51. v. l. *aiwisrūθrəm ananąm*.

aiwiš N. 4.

aiwišantō N. 52.

aiwištāra Phl. Vd. 1. 19.

aiwišti cf. *an°*.

aiwištəm N. 4.

aiwizuš Phl. Vd. 5. 32.

aiwi-xᵛarənti Vij. p. 136.

aiwegāma N. 48.

aiwyaṇhaṭ N. 16.

aiwyaṇhəm N. 10.

aiwyast[čiṭ N. 51.

aiwyāiti T. 65.

aiwyāiš N. 14 (2).

aiwyāxšayāṭ N. 77.

aiwyāsta N. 85 ; Yt. (Vtp.) 24. 23.

aiwyāstāṭ N. 83.

aiwvāsti N. 2, 15.

aiwyāstiš N. 9.

aiwyāstəm N. 87, 96 ; Yt. (Vtp.)
24. 23.

aiwyāstō N. 37, 86, 87 (2); T.
10. Cf. *an°*.

aiwyāstąm N. 95 (2).

aiwyāstrəm N. 96.

aiwyō N. 48, 71 ; T. 32 ; Vij.
p. 165 ; W. 7. 1.

aiwyåŋha[*ča* N. 94.

aiwyåŋhaṯ N. 11.

aiwyåŋhana N. 95, 108.

aiwiyåŋhanašnī Vij. p. 186.

aiwyåŋhanō Vij. p. 138 (2).

aiwyåŋhayeāite N. 87.

aiwyåŋhavånti N. 85, 91 (2),
92, 93.

aiwyåŋhānō Vij. p. 160, 181.

aiwvå[*nayå*]*nti* N. 85.

aiwyånti N. 93.

[*aiwyåsti*] v. l. N. 2.

aiŋhå Phl. Vd. 2. 32 ; 3. 40; 7.
52.

ain N. 72, 81, 83.

aina T. 38.

ainaidkim N. 66. (v. l. *ainid-
kim*.)

ainikō ZPGl. 7. 13.

ainitiš T. 53.

ainitōiṯ ZPGl. 20. 1.

ainitōiš ZPGl. 20. 1.

ainim N. 1.

ainisritīm N. 10.

ainištiš T. 12.

ainəm N. 11.

ainye N. 60.

ainyche N. 25.

ainyō N. 24, 63 ; T. 121 (2).

airišta N. 56.

airištō ZPGl. 20. 2.

airyanəmna N. 103.

airvanąm cf. *an°*.

airyamanəm W. 4. 1 (2).

airišyā N. 67.

airyəmā N. 36; Phl. Ys. 27 end.

auruša-bāzvō Yt. 22. 9 ; Yt.
(Vtp.) 24. 56.

aurvaθanąm Yt. (Vtp.) 24. 25.
Cf. *aourvat°*.

aurvaṯ ZPGl. 21. 1.

aurvaṯ-aspā[*ča* Yt. (Vtp.) 24.
34, 46.

aurvaṯ-aspəm Yt. (APZ.) 23. 6.

aurvaš N. 15.

aēāvišti N. 15 (v. l. *aēnav°* and
anāv°).

aēiti W. 8. 2 (2).

aēiθāhu[*ča* Yt. 22. 25.

aēibyō N. 20, 107 ; T. 27 ; Yt.
(Vtp.) 24. 35.

aēta N. 2, 71, 84 ; T. 45, 79 ;
Yt. 22. 14 (3) ; Yt. (Vtp.) 24.
60 (3) ; ZPGl. 17. 10.

aētaēibyō N. 108.

aētaēšąm N. 33, 37, 52, 53, 63,
67, 82, 83, 109 (2) ; Vij. p.
23, 89.

aētaδa N. 11, 26 (2), 71 ; Phl.
Vd. 4. 49.

aētaṯ N. 46, 47, 65, 70 ; Pars.
p. 534 ; Vij. p. 179 ; Vth. 24 ;
Yt. (Vtp.) 24. 22, 26.

aētaŋhå N. 67.

aētaṋhąm N. 63.

aētaya N. 53, 81.

aētayå N. 90.

aētava[tō] N. 87.

aētavatō N. 21, 23, 39.

aētavaṯ N. 108, 109. Cf. bis°.

aētavaṯ[ča N. 12.

aētavō N. 21.

aētahe N. 11 (2), 70 (2), 87 (2), 105 ; Phl. Vd. 5. 9; 7. 52 ; T. 117 ; Vij. p. 89, 179 (2).

aētahmāi N. 18, 61, 62.

aētahmāṯ N. 4, 9, 70, 87.

aētahmi T. 78, 87, 99.

aētahmya N. 12.

aētāibyō N. 71.

aēti N. 67, 80.

aētəm Ep. M. 1. 4. 3 ; N. 82 ; T. 79; Vij. p. 145, 148, 180, 181 ; ZPGl. 43. 4.

aētōe N. 29, 33, 108, 109; ZPGl. 7. 8.

aēte N. 52, 61 (in dātāčaaēte), 64 (4) ; Phl. Vd. 4. 1 ; Vij. p. 160, 179, 180 ; ZPGl. 15. 2.

aētenōiš Yt. 22. 13 (v. l. Haug and West, Arda Viraf. avač-nōiš).

aētå N. 71.

aētåsete N. 65 (read aētåsə tē ?)

aētąm N. 28, 103 ; Phl. Vd. 3. 14 ; Yt. 22. 1, 2, 3, 19, 20 ; Yt. (Vtp.) 24. 53.

aētąm[čiṯ Yt. 22. 4, 6.

aētyavantəm Yt. (Vtp.) 24. 63.

aētyąm[čiṯ T. 25.

aētšaya ZPGl. 41. 5.

aēθrapaitinąm N. 13.

aēθrapaitim N. 11, 12, cf. aiθ°.

aēθrapaitiš HtN. p. 483 ; ZPGl. 21. 2.

aēθrapaitīm N. 10.

aēθrapatayō A. 59.

aēθrapatōiṯ N. 16.

aēθraya N. 46.

aēθrayāi N. 17.

aēða N. 51 ; ZPGl. 6. 11, 12.

aēnaṋhe Pars. p. 540.

[aēnavišti] v. l. N. 15.

aēništəm N. 109.

aēnəm N. 44, 45.

aēnyāi[čiṯ N. 57. Cf. paē° corrupt.

aēnyō N. 107.

aēm N. 27 (2) ; Phl. Vd. 1. 14.

aēmaṯ N. 12 (read aēm aṯ).

aēm[ča Phl. Vd. 1. 14.

aēm[čiṯ Phl. Vd. 2. 5.

[aēyąm] v. l. Phl. Vd. 3. 14.

aēva A. 51 ; N. 103 ; Vij. p. 158 ; W. Yt. 21. 5, 6, 8, 10, 12, 14, 16 ; Yt. (APZ.) 23. 2, 5 ; Yt. (Vtp.) 24. 3.

aēvatō N. 38.

aēvaθa N. 11.

aēvaða N. 80.

aēvaya[čiṯ T. 40 (2).

aēvayaya[čiṯ N. 103.

aēvahe N. 22, 65.

aēvahmi W. Yt. 21. 1.

aēvākəm Vij. p. 139.

aēvāčina N. 5.

aēve N. 103.

aēvō A. 77, 78, 79, 80, 81 ; HtN. p. 484; N. 46, 60, 81; Phl. Vd. **5**. 34; T. 68 (2), 99; Vij. p. 133, 191 ; ZPGl. 7. 5.

aēvōjanō A. 80.

aēvō-baɣəm Vij. p. 24 (2).

aēvąm N. 42, 43, 65, 74.

aēsayå Yt. (Vtp.) **24**. 41.

aēsma[*ča* N. 105, 108.

aēsmahe N. 106.

aēsmi N. 28.

aēsməm N. 103.

aēsmō-bərəite T. 40.

aēsmąn cf. *dāityō*°.

aēsmąs[*ča* N. 71.

aēša Ep. M. **1**. 4. 3; N. 3, 7, 9, 17, 103.

aēšaya N. 3 (2).

aēšayamanąm N. 68.

aēšas[*čiṯ* N. 12.

aēšā N. 7.

aēšəntəm ZPGl. 16. 5.

aēšō Ep. M. **1**. 4. 3 ; N. 2, 19, 24, 60, 69, 70, 90, 103 ; T. 53 ; Vij. p. 126, 136; W. Yt. **21**. 4 ; Yt. **22**. 41 (2).

aēšąm N. 29, 52, 53, 61, 62, 85, 89, 103 ; Phl. Vd. **7**. 72 ; T. 30 ; Yt. **22**. 40 ; Yt. (Vtp.) **24**. 30, 34, 35, 39, 42 (2). Cf. also *hačaṯ*°.

aēšåm[*ča* Phl. Vd. **5**. 9.

aēšmahe Pars. p. 535.

aēšməm W. **9**. 2.

aouye Vij. p. 138 (read *duye*).

aourvatanąm Yt. (Vtp.) **24**. 19 (read *aurvaθ*°).

aoxta Vij. p. 138, 180 ; W. Yt. **21**. 2, 7, 9, 11, 13, 15, 17 ; Yt. **22**. 10, 16, 34, 40 ; Yt. (APZ.) **23**. 1 ; Yt. (Vtp.) **24**. 24, 54, 55, 57, 62. Cf. *paiti*°.

aoxte N. 7, 9, 19 ; ZPGl. 14. 4.

aoxtō N. 7 (2).

aoxtō-nāmanō Vij. p. 141.

aogəmadaē[*ča* A. 1.

aoge N. 108 v. l. *aō*° (read *aēvō* ?).

aojaiti Phl. Vd. **8**. 80.

aojaṇha Phl. Vd. **15**. 10.

aojas[*ča* Pars. p. 531.

aojastarō Phl. Vd. **4**. 10.

aojištəm Yt. (APZ.) **23**. 3. Cf. also *ašaojišta*.

aojīta Yt. (Vtp.) **24**. 11.

aojəmna Yt. **22**. 42.

aojō-rāmištąm Phl. Vd. **1**. 1.

aoθrəmahe Phl. Vd. **3**. 15.

aodra N. 15 (2).

aom Yt. **22**. 38.

aora Phl. Vd. **2**. 40 ; ZPGl. 21. 1.

aošaṇuhaiti A. 48.

aošaṇuhatąm A. 58.

aošaṇhaṯ Phl. Vd. **2**. 5 (2).

aošaṇhå A. 48 ; Phl. Vd. **2**. 5.

aošantā Yt. (Vtp.) **24**. 40.

aošante W. **8**. 1.

aošəm Phl. Vd. **8**. 74.

aoštra ZPGl. 8. 3.

ạošnarō Yt. (APZ.) **23**. 2.

aōi T. 14, 35, 38, 62, 82.

aōmǝm W. **9**. 2.

aōyamnāṭ T. 55.

aōyǝmnǝm T. 55.

akaranahe Yt. (Vtp.) **24**. 24.

akǝrǝnaoṭ Phl. Vd. **2**. 5.

akyåsčaṇha N. 103.

axtǝm N. 15.

aʌtō N. 20 (read *haʌtō*).

axšaēnō A. 78, 79.

agǝnyå Phl. Ys. **38**. 13 (Sp.).

aɣa ZPGl. 20, 9.

aɣaurvaya N. 54.

aɣa-daēna Yt. (APZ.) **23**. 3.

aɣā Phl. Vd. **3**. 15.

aɣǝm Phl. Vd. **19**. 30.

aɣra ZPGl. 20. 9.

aɣraēšva cf. *an°.*

aɣrišyā Yt. (Vtp.). **24**. 29.

aɣrǝm ZPGl. 20. 9; 43. 1.

aɣryehe T. 65.

aɣryō N. 45; T. 65.

aɣryōtǝmō ZPGl. 12. 1.

ačiθō ZPGl. 20. 2.

ačiθōirištǝm N. 29.

ačiθrō ZPGl. 20. 3.

ačištǝm T. 16; W. **3**. 2.

ačištэe N. 62.

ajiθō FD. 7.

aθa A. 111; AG. 10; N. 8, 9, 10, 37, 42 (3), 43, 44, 46, 65 (2), 68 (2), 70, 83, 93, 99, 108 (3); SkN. p. 480; T. 10, 27; Vij. p. 137; Vth.

11; Yt. (APZ.) **23**. 8; Yt. (Vtp.) **24**. 31 (2); ZPGl. 12. 10; 20. 8; 38. 6.

aθaurunǝm N. 1, 3, 4, 5, 6, 7.

aθaurunō Yt. (APZ.) **23**. 5; Yt. (Vtp.) **24**. 3, 16.

aθaurunąm [*ča* N. 4.

aθauronō ZPGl. 21. 9.

aθavaθa N. 92. (D. reads *aθaraθa*.)

aθā N. 37 (2), 46, 60, 68, 72, 73, .103; Phl. Vd. **9**. 27; T. 6; Vij. p. 152.

aθāhva T. 107.

aθwǝrǝsaya N. 105.

aθra Yt. (Vtp.) **24**. 35, 43.

aθrava N. 4.

aθrāṭ N. 58.

aθrāvayaṭ A. 81.

aθrāvayō N. 104.

adaδāiti T. 3.

adavata Yt. **22**. 35.

adasta Yt. (Vtp.) **24**. 39.

adā W. **8**. 2.

aδa A. 53; FD. 3; N. 10, 53; Phl. Vd. **1**. 3 (2), 14–15 (2); ZPGl. 20. 8.

aδairi N. 85.

[*aδaue*] v. l. (D.) Phl. Ys. **64** 48 (Sp.).

aδaē [*ča* N. 37.

aδa [*ča* Phl. Vd. **7**. 52.

aδaṇ [*aṇ*]*he* N. 55.

aδayāṭ N. 72, 73.

aδarō ZPGl. **9**. 12.

aδāiti N. 54; T. 119.

aδāitya N. 18.

aδāityō N. 17, 107.

aδāityō-xratuš Yt. (Vtp.) 24. 44.

aδāityō-draonaṃhas [ča N. 52.

aδāṯ N. 60, 71 (2); Vij. p. 181 ; Yt. 22. 37 ; ZPGl. 21. 10.

aδi N. 46.

aδwā N. 15.

aδwāityas [ča N. 9.

aṯ N. 36, 70, 92 ; Pars. p. 540 ; Phl. Vd. 11. 20 (= 11. 41 Sp.); Phl. Ys. 27 end ; T. 4, 28, 30, 46, 50, 55 (2), 61, 65, 70 (2) ; Vij. p. 126, 133. Cf. *aēmaṯ* N. 12.

aṯ [ča T. 31.

aṯbištō Yt. (Vtp.) 24. 38.

apa N. 54, 71, 78, 103, 108 ; Pars. p. 540, 541 (2) ; Yt. (Vtp.) 24. 44 ; ZPGl. 4. 3.

apaita N. 54.

apaiti N. 54.

upuitij ni FD. 7.

apaitirita ZPGl. 11. 9.

apaitiš-xᵛarǝθā̊ Yt. (Vtp.) 24. 38.

apaityānō N. 55.

apairi A. 81.

apairiayō A. 57.

apairiθwō A 77, 78, 79, 80, 81.

apaē [čiṯ N. 69.

apaxtaraēibyō Yt. 22. 25. Cf. *apā°*.

apagayehē Phl. Ys. 17. 55 ; 32. 5 (Sp.); 41. 7 (Sp.); 42. 1 (Sp.); 45. 4 (Sp.); 52. 6, 8 (Sp.); 60. 10 (Sp.).

apa-jasō Yt. 22. 16, 34 ; Yt. (Vtp.) 24. 62.

apaθatō FD. 7.

[*apaθrǝstǝmǝmčaṯ*] v. l. for *upaθ°* N. 51.

apaṯāta T. 101.

apaṃhabdǝnti N. 52.

apanasyehe Pars. p. 541.

apantąm HtN. p. 484.

apayaēiti N. 33.

apayaēša N. 109.

apayanta N. 32.

apayāiti N. 42 (2).

apayeiti N. 12.

apayą ZPGl. 11. 12.

apara Yt. (Vtp.) 24. 48.

aparaoθǝmnahe N. 54.

aparaṯ N. 37 ; Yt. (Vtp.) 24. 29.

aparaya ZPGl. 7. 1.

aparāδǝm [ča Vij. p. 96.

upurǝm N. 44.

apare A. 53.

aparąm N. 79.

apas [ča N. 48, 50 ; T. 115 ; Vij. p. 165 ; W. 7. 1 ; Yt. 22, 13 ; Yt. (Vtp.) 24. 59.

apastūitiš N. 41.

apastāiṯ N. 41.

apašūtōiṯ T. 39.

apāxǝδre Pars. p. 541.

apāʌtaraēibyō Yt. 22. 25, 42. Cf. *apa°*.

apāxtaraṯ Yt. 22. 25, 42.
api-gərəftayāṯ N. 17.
apipyūšinąm Yt. (Vtp.) 24. 50.
apuθra Vij. p. 158.
apuθrāi Vij. p. 25.
apuθrīm Vij. p. 179.
apuyąn Yt. (Vtp.) 24. 45.
apəmō ZPGl. 20. 4.
apəm [*ča* N. 47.
apəm [*čiṯ* Phl. Vd. 18. 2.
apərənahe Phl. Vd. 8. 22.
apərənāyuka ZPGl. 4. 6.
apərənāyukanąm ZPGl. 4. 7.
apərənāyukō ZPGl. 4. 6.
apərənāyunąm N. 11, 105.
apərənāyūka N. 9, 11.
apərənāyūkahe N. 7.
apərənāyūkahe [*čiṯ* N. 40.
apərənāyūkāi N. 7.
apərənāyūkō N. 7. 9, 10 ; Vij. p. 160.
apərənāyūkm N. 105 (read °*kəm.*).
apərənāyūbyō N. 11.
apərənāyōiš N. 54.
apərəmnōi N. 13.
apərəyūkō N. 10.
ape N. 67 (2), 69.
apō N. 26, 70 ; Yt. (Vtp.) 24. 31.
apōi N. 26.
apōiṯ N. 26.
[*apōtəməm*] v. l. N. 12.
apąm N. 20, 47, 48 (3) ; Vij. p. 89, 165 (2) ; W. 7. 1 (2).
apnō cf. *hapsnāi°*.

apnōtəm N. 12.
apvatie ZPGl. 20. 4.
afiθyō ZPGl. 11. 12.
afraōxte N. 13.
afračičīš T. 101.
afradərəsavantəm A. 28.
aframarənti N. 22.
aframarəntəm N. 53.
afravaočīš T. 101.
afravaōčō N. 14.
afrasaṇhąn [*ča* T. 83.
afrašāvayō N. 103.
afrityō Yt. (Vth.) 24. 45.
afrəraiti Yt. (Vtp.) 24. 30.
afrōti N. 13 (read *afraoxti*).
afryō-zaotārō Yt. (Vtp.) 24. 12.
afsmainiivąn [*ča* N. 24.
afsmainya N. 23.
afsmainyąn N. 24.
aba N. 10.
abavaṯ Yt. 22. 16 ; Yt. (Vtp.) 24. 62.
abanta N. 56.
abarəšnvu Phl. Vd. 2. 5.
awra ZPGl. 21. 1.
aṇuha N. 7, 15 ; Vij. p. 23.
aṇuhi Vij. p. 126.
aṇuhe Yt. (Vtp.) 24. 33.
aṇra N. 15.
aṇra mainyavō Yt. (Vtp.) 24. 37.
aṇras [*ča* Yt. (Vtp.) 24. 47.
aṇrahe Pars. p. 535 ; T. 37.
aṇrahe mainyōuš HtN. p. 484.
aṇrāi A. 28.

aᶇrō mainyuš A. 28; Phl. Vd.
18. 2; W. 4. 2, 3; Yt. 22.
35; Yt. (Vtp.) 24. 43.

aᶇha N. 59; Yt. (Vtp.) 24. 50.

aᶇhaoṯ Yt. 22. 16 (2), 34 (2);
Yt. (Vtp.) 24. 33, 62 (2).

aᶇhaṯ N. 9, 17, 31, 45, 68,
72; Phl. Vd. 1. 14; T. 23,
98; Vij. p. 24, 25, 158; Vth.
2, 5, 15; W. 8. 2 (2); Yt·
22. 34; Yt. (Vtp.) 24. 30.

aᶇhavanəm[ča N. 72.

aᶇhavō cf. *duž°*.

aᶇhuī W. 3. 2. Cf. next word.

aᶇhuīm W. 3. 2 (2).

aᶇhunąm Yt. (Vtp.) 24. 30.

aᶇhum cf. *daož°*.

aᶇhuyaṯ T. 62; W. Yt. 21. 3.

aᶇhuš T. 92; Yt. 22. 2, 20;
ZPGl. 11. 11.

aᶇhən N. 8, 46, 90, 108; Vij.
p. 126; W. 1. 1.

aᶇhən[ča N. 60.

aᶇhəm ZPGl. 15. 3.

aᶇhōuš A. 28, 69; N. 63, 84,
T. 14, 58, 90, 91, 98, 108;
Vij. p. 151; Yt. (Vtp.) 24. 32
(2), 36, 48; ZPGl. 40. 7.

aᶇhe N. 8 (2), 72; T. 22 (2),
87, 109; Yt. (Vtp.) 24. 30,
38.

aᶇhō Phl. Vd. 5. 9.

aᶇhå A. 66 ; W. 8. 1 ; Yt. 22.
9; Yt. (Vtp.) 24. 42, 56;
ZPGl. 40.6.

aᶇhrō FD. 7.

aᶇhvō T. 78, 87, 99.

aᶇhvąm Phl. Vd. 5. 19.

ana N. 80; T. 37, 38; Yt.
(Vtp.) 24. 39, 49 (2), 50 (2).

anaiwiərətavō N. 79.

anaiwišti N. 14.

anaiwištīm N. 4.

anaiwyāsta N. 85, 95.

anaiwyāsti N. 95, 96.

anaiwyāstō N. 96.

anairyanąm N. 68.

anaivišti N. 15.

anaomō HtN. p. 485.

anakåse N. 63. cf. *anā°*.

anaᴀtō N. 7.

anaɣra AG. 7.

anaɣraēšva Yt. 22. 15, 27–33 ;
Yt. (Vtp.) 24. 61.

anaɣra[ča T. 83.

anaɣrā ZPGl. 20. 1.

anadya N. 56.

anabdātəm Yt. (Vtp.) 24. 23.

anawišti N. 14.

anaᶇrō N. 15.

anuᶇhuṯ Vij. p. 29.

ananąm v. l. N. 51 (in
aiwisrūθrəmananąm).

anantarə N. 83.

anamarəždikahe A. 77, 78, 79,
80, 81.

anamarəždikō A. 78, 79, 80.

anamasna[ča T. 94 (read *ana-
masana*[ča cf. Yt. 19. 58).

anavahīm T. 118.

anasčaiti N. 109.

anastāiš[ča N. 57.

anastritəm N. 10(v. l. anistritim).
anašavanəm N. 109.
anazayanąm N. 58.
anazdya N. 56.
anazyāiš N. 57 (2).
anahaxti N. 80.
anahaxtō N. 6 (2), 63.
anahmāṭ N. 99.
anaʜvāstāiš N. 57.
anā N. 9; W. 9. 1.
anākåse N. 6. cf. ana°.
anāxštō W. 9. 1.
anāpərəθa Vij. p. 25.
anāmarəždikō A. 49.
anāmāta ZPGl. 19. 10.
[anāvišti] v. l. N. 15.
anāstərətō N. 46, 50 (v. l. °star°).
anāstravanəm Yt. (APZ.) 23. 3.
anāhita ZPGl. 19. 5.
anisriš N. 10.
anu N. 25, 89, 103.
anutačaite N. 7.
anumaiti N. 25.
anumayanąm W. Yt. 21. 5.
anusaiti N. 6.
anusaityti[ča N. 6.
anusvå N. 107.
anušō Ep. M. 1. 4. 3 (2).
anåʜhō T. 16.
anguštąm Vij. p. 138.
anta N. 107.
antara N. 101.
antaraṭ N. 60.
antarāṭ N. 11 (2), 69 (2), 94, 104 (2); Phl. Vd. 2. 40.

antarə N. 40, 65, 67, 68, 83 (4), 94 (2), 97, 103, 109; Phl. Vd. 18. 70; T. 61, 63, 75, 76, 77; Vij. p. 145, 146; ZPGl. 41. 6.
antarə[ča Vij. p. 148; W. Yt. 21. 16 (2).
antarəm N. 91.
antəma Vij. p. 138.
anya N. 109; Vij. p. 88, 188; Vth. 13.
anyaēibyō Yt. 22. 7, 25; Yt. (Vtp.) 24. 45, 55.
anyaēm Pars. p. 540.
anyaēšąm HtN. p. 484; N. 83; Phl. Vd. 19. 25; SlS. 13. 8; W. Yt. 21. 6, 8, 10, 12; Yt. 22. 37.
anya-ṭkaēša Vth. 17. Cf. anyō°.
anyahe N. 6.
anyāiš N. 47.
anyāhu N. 102.
anye A. 69; ZPGl. 7. 8.
anyehe N. 7, 101, 104; Yt. (Vtp.) 24. 36.
anyō N. 18, 25, 61, 62; Phl. Vd. 5. 2; 13. 9 = 13. 24 (Sp.).
anyō-ṭkaēša Vth. 3, 8. Cf. anya°.
anyå N. 46, 50.
anyąm[ča N. 92.
ama N. 28.
amana ZPGl. 19. 10.
amaya Yt. 22. 9; Yt. (Vtp.) 24. 56.
amarātanąm N. 58.

amarəždika- cf. *an°.*
amaršą ZPGl. 11. 12.
amava Yt. (APZ.) 23. 2.
amavaiti Yt. (Vtp.) 24. 22.
amavata ZPGl. 8. 12.
amavantəm Yt. (Vtp.) 24. 42.
amavå Yt. (Vtp.) 24. 2.
amahe N. 47 ; W. 5. 1.
amahe[*ča* W. Yt. 21. 4.
amahrka Yt. (Vtp.) 24. 4.
amahrkəm Yt. (APZ.) 23. 7.
amā FD. 7.
aməm Yt. (Vtp.) 24. 6, 39.
aməm[*ča* Pars. p. 531 ; W. 5. 2.
amərətaṯbya W. Yt. 21. 7.
amərətāta N. 28 (3).
amərətatəm Vij. p. 52.
amərəza Phl. Ys. 9. 4.
aməša N. 20, 28, 46, 65, 71 ;
   ZPGl. 19. 10.
aməšaēibyō Phl. Vd. 19. 25.
aməša[*čiṯ* A. 41. (v. l.
   hamas[*čiṯ*).
aməšanąm CB; Vij. p. 141,
   181 ; W. 1. 2; 5. 1; Yt.
   (Vtp.) 24. 46.
aməšā N. 46; SlS. 13. 1 ; Vij.
   p. 152; W. 5. 2; Yt. (Vtp.)
   24. 32, 40.
aməšəm Pars. p. 531.
aməšə̄ Vij. p. 53, 128.
aməšə̄sa T. 76.
aməšə̄-spəntə̄ N. 70; Yt. (Vtp.)
   24. 12.
amå FD. 7.
amąsta ZPGl. 7. 7.

amraxsąn Yt. (Vtp.) 24. 45.
amhāi ZPGl. 20. 7.
aya N. 54.
ayaōxšustahe Dk. (P. Sj.) 3. 156.
aya[*ča* Yt. (Vtp.) 24. 51.
ayaptō-dātəmas[*ča* T. 109.
ayaṇhaṯ Vij. p. 29.
ayaṇhanaēibya N. 107.
ayaṇhana[*ča* Vij. p. 83.
ayanəm N. 9.
ayantu CB.
ayara N. 47 (2) ; Vij. p. 126,
   179, 184.
ayaranąm Vij. p. 148, 157, 179.
ayaranąm[*ča* N. 47 ; Vij. p.
   126, 137, 179.
ayarə A. 51 ; N. 42, 43, 69 (2),
   83, 109; ZPGl. 42. 4 ; 43. 1.
ayarə̄ A. 53.
ayarna cf. *uz°.*
ayasaṇha Yt. (Vtp.) 24. 9.
ayaska Yt. (Vtp.) 24. 4.
ayaskəm Yt. (APZ.) 23. 7.
ayasnīm AG. 5.
ayazəmna Yt. (Vtp.) 24. 12.
ayeni Yt. 22. 20 ; Yt. (Vtp.)
   24. 65.
ayå N. 8.
ayąn A. 53 (2) ; Yt. (Vtp.) 24.
   30.
araityåntō Yt. (Vtp.) 24. 5.
aratuxšaθrayāi Yt. 22. 36.
aratufriš N. 25, 37 (2), 55, 100,
   101 (2), 102 (2), 104, 105
   (2), 108 (2).
aratu[*friš*] N. 22.

[a]ratufriš N. 55 (2).
aratufrya N. 24, 32.
aratufryō N. 33, 39, 87, 88, 91,
92, 93, 94, 95, 97.
aratō-kərəθinō ZPGl. 21. 2.
aratvō T. 16.
araθwya Yt. (Vtp.) 24. 47 (2),48.
araθwyō-bərəte T. 47.
araθwyō-varšti T. 57. (read
raθwyō°).
araduša N. 15, 42.
aranhąm Yt. (Vtp.) 24. 2.
arastrəm N. 32.
arāθraoṯ N. 78.
arāṯ N. 71.
ariz Bd. 14. 26 (is this Avestan? Cf. SBE. 5. 51 and 47.
160 note).
arura ZPGl. 20. 10.
arəjaiti W. Yt. 21. 5, 6, 8, 10,
12, 14, 16.
arəjō N. 85 ; ZPGl. 12. 2.
arəθavanō ZPGl. 43. 8.
arəθnå ZPGl. 10.2.
arəθra ZPGl. 17. 10.
arəduməm N. 65.
arədušāṯ N. 54.
arədvaē N. 85 (v. l. aredvāē).
arədvō-zəngō Phl. Vd. 5. 9.
arədaṅha N. 65.
arənå FD. 7.
arənti cf. frər°.
arəm T. 46 (3) ; ZPGl. 21. 2.
Cf. also bis° and θrəs°.
arəmōidō N. 103.
arəšō A. 79.

arəna ZPGl. 21. 1.
arå̄nti W. 4. 1. Cf. paiti°.
arduš N. 45.
armaitī N. 46.
armō T. 68.
aršuxδa Phl. Ys. 9. 25.
aršuxδanąm [ča N. 46.
arštištim N. 2.
arštīm T. 34.
arštå N. 44.
arš-ṯkaēšəm Yt. (APZ.) 23. 7.
aršvačastəmāi N. 80.
arzukā Bd. 14. 26.
arzuvā Bd. 14. 26 ; Zsp. 22. 4.
ava N. 16, 42 (2), 43, 52, 54,
v. l. 67, 100, 101, 102 ; T.
35 (2), 38, 68, 81, 122 ; W.
8. 2 ; Yt. 22. 11, 12, 16 (2) ;
Yt. (Vtp.) 24. 43, 49, 58.
ava(i) Vij. p. 179.
avaiaṯ ZPGl. 21. 9
avaiti Phl. Vd. 2. 19.
avaətå ZPGl. 30. 8.
avaēpaēm Phl. Vd. 1. 2 (2).
[avaēnōiš] v. l. Yt. 22. 13. (for
aētenōiš).
avaēšąm ZPGl. 12. 7.
avaēzō AG. 10 ; N. 67 (3).
ava[ča W. Yt. 21. 16.
avačinō N. 5.
avačō-urvaitīm AG. 7.
avačyō N. 24.
ava-janəm W. 8. 1.
avaθa A. 19 ; N. 68 ; Phl. Vd.
2. 32 ; Vij. p. 24 ; W. 8. 2 ;
Yt. (Vtp.) 24. 27, 42, 54.

ava-θwarǝsahe ZPGl. 35. 9.
avaδa N. 15 ; Phl. Vd. 4. 49 ;
   Yt. 22. 20.
avaṯ Ep. M. 1. 4. 3 ; N. 3, v. l.
   50 ; Phl. Vd. 7. 52 ; T. 1, 34,
   35, 48 ; Vij. p. 25 ; Yt. (Vtp.)
   24. 29, 46 ; ZPGl. 13. 2.
avapa N. 2.
avabarāṯ N. 65.
avabarǝtąm ZPGl. 16. 7.
ava-barǝnti N. 93.
avanuhabdǝmnō W. Yt. 21. 11.
avanrāsayāṯ N. 85.
avanha N. 54.
avanhabdǝmnō N. 53.
avanhas[*ča* T. 100.
avanhō A. 41.
avanhā̊ Vij. p. 141.
avanǝmnanąm Yt. (Vtp.) 24. 6.
ava-mairyanuha Yt. 22. 34 ;
   Yt. (Vtp.) 24. 62.
ava-mairyeite Yt. 22. 19.
ava-mīryaēšaēiti W. 8. 1.
ava-mīryāite W. 8. 1, 2.
ava-mǝrǝitīm Yt. 22. 36 (2);
   Vt. (Vtp.) 24. 64.
ava-mǝrǝtō Yt. 22. 34.
avayāṯ ZPGl. 21. 10.
avayō N. 84.
avayā̊ N. 11.
avarǝ ZPGl. 20. 3.
avarǝta ZPGl. 16. 1.
avarǝt(*a*)*nąm* Vij. p. 23, 24, 158.
avava T. 38.
avavata Phl. Vd. 15. 10 ; T.
   37.

avavatō Yt. 22. 9 ; Yt. (Vtp.)
   24. 56.
avavaṯ N. 69 ; Yt. 22. 2, 4, 6,
   20.
avavaṯ[*čiṯ* Phl. Vd. 7. 52 ; Vij.
   p. 148.
avavāite T. 117.
avastātǝm ZPGl. 9. 3.
avaspayama Yt. (Vtp.) 24. 44.
avāi N. 58.
avāunhieiti ZPGl. 35. 4.
avāhi Yt. (Vtp.) 24. 4. (*ba-*
   vāhi ?)
avi N. 67 ; Phl. Vd. 8. 74 ; SlS.
   13. 8 ; Vij. p. 23, 24, 89 (3),
   116, 126 (3), 128 (2), 138,
   139, 146, 148, 157, 158, 160
   (2), 181 (2) ; W.Yt. 21. 3 ;
   Yt. 22. 34 (2). Yt. (Vtp.) 24.
   62 (2).
avī N. 98.
ave Ep. M. 1. 4. 3.
avō W. 8. 2.
avōiṯ N. 2, 3.
avō-dātǝm Yt. (Vtp.) 24. 23.
avōya Yt. 22. 34.
avā̊ N. 46, 50, 54.
avąn N. 9.
as Phl. Vd. 2. 19 ; ZPGl. 20. 5.
asaočantaṯ N. 58.
asayāiti T. 24.
asānaēnaēibya N. 108.
asāra Phl. Vd. 2. 5.
asǝvištā̊ A. 59.
asō Phl. Vd. 1. 1 ; Yt. (Vtp.)
   24. 29.

asta ZPGl. 20. 5.

asta-išum ZPGl. 20. 6.

astaēnaēibya N. 107.

astaoθwanəm [*čā* SlS. **13**. 1.

asta [*ča* T. 35.

astarənti N. 95.

astarəm T. 79.

astavaitīm Vij. p. 25.

astavaintəm Vij. p. 126.

astavanti T. 78 ; Vij. p. 23.

astas [*ča* Yt. **22.** 17, 35 ; Yt. (Vtp.) **24.** 63.

astātō ZPGl. 20. 3.

astāraiti N. 67.

asti A. 49 ; N. 30, 47, 109 (2), Phl. Vd. **13.** 9 (= 24 Sp.) ; SkN. p. 480 ; T. 27, 54 ; Vth. 7 ; Yt. **22.** 18, 36 ; Yt. (Vtp.) **24.** 4, 31, 32, 49, 64 ; ZPGl. 17. 9 ; 38. 5 ; 43. 1. Cf. also *paiti*° and *parō*°.

astiš [*ča* T. 37.

astī N. 39 (2) ; Phl. Vd. **19.** 18 (2) ; T. 113.

astəm ZPGl. 7. 5 ; 11. 5.

astō T. 97.

astōvīδōtuš A. 57.

astryehe ZPGl. 15. 11.

astvaiti Yt. (Vtp.) **24.** 38.

astvaitinąm W. Yt. **21.** 1 ; Yt. **22.** 1.

astvaitīš Pars. p. 541 ; Phl. Vd. **8.** 72 ; **9.** 27.

astvaite T. 87.

astvainti T. 87.

astvaēitibyō T. 15.

astvataṯ Yt. **22.** 16, 34 ; Yt. (Vtp.) **24.** 62.

astvatahe T. 90.

astvatō N. 63, 84 ; T. 14, 58, 98 ; Yt. (Vtp.) **24.** 36 ; ZPGl. 40. 7.

astvanti T. 99.

astvahe T. 91.

astvāiti N. 72.

astvā̆ W. **4.** 3 ; ZPGl. 11. 11.

aspa A. 84 ; Vij. p. 125 ; Yt. (Vtp.) **24.** 29, 48. Cf. *kərəsā*° and *pouru*°.

aspaṇhāδō A. 78.

aspayanąm N. 67.

aspayāaṯ [*ča* N. 67.

aspayā̆ N. 85.

aspahe N. 58 ; Vij. p. 83 ; Yt. (Vtp.) **24.** 35 ; ZPGl. 15. 10.

aspəm A. 82, cf. *aurvaṯ*°.

aspərənāyūkahe [*ča* N. 40 (v. l. *apərenayūkahe* [*čiṯ*).

aspərənō N. 23 (2), 91, 96 ; ZPGl. 20. 4.

aspərənąm Vij. 97, 132.

aspərəzō-dātəmas [*ča* T. 109.

aspō N. 37, 47 ; Phl. Vd. **6.** 26 ; ZPGl. 12. 1.

aspkərəntō N. 96 (read *as- pərənō*).

aspyā N. 30.

asnāaṯ [*ča* Yt. **22.** 13 ; Yt. (Vtp.) **24.** 59.

asni Yt. **22.** 38.

asne T. 33 ; Yt. **22.** 2, 20 ; Yt. (Vtp.) **24.** 54.

asnya N. 47.

asnyaṇąm [ča N. 47.

asnye Vij. p. 88, 188.

asmana[ča Vij. p. 83.

asmanəm W. Yt. 21. 16.

[asma-rəja] v. l. Phl. Vd. 18. 70.

asməm N. 103, v. l. asməmə (read aēsməm); Vij. p. 5.

asmō-x°anvå Yt. 22. 37.

asraōšyanąm T. 18.

asrasčintəm N. 68.

asrāvayamnåṯ N. 68.

asrāvayō N. 41, 42 (2), 43, 44 (2), 45.

asriti N. 11.

asruiti N. 30.

asruti N. 30.

asrutəm N. 103.

asrutå N. 25.

asruṯ-gaošō N. 14.

as-hya N. 101.

aša Phl. Ys. 95 end(Sp.); T. 94, 103; Yt. (Vtp.) 24. 42.

ašaunąm [ča Pars. p. 534.

ašaēta W. 3. 2 (2).

ašaojišta W. 8. 2.

ašaoni Phl. Vd. 2. 19.

ašaonīš N. 103; T. 77.

ašaone N. 15, 16, 84; Phl. Vd. 19. 18; Yt. (Vtp.) 24. 22, 27, 36.

ašaonō N. 46, 47, 81; Pars. p. 535; Phl. Vd. 2. 5; 3. 15, 40 (2); T. 44, 74, 89, 120. Vij. p. 128; W. 1. 1; 2. 1;

9. 3; W. Yt. 21. 5; Yt. 22. 7, 8, 10, 15 (4), 37; Yt. (Vtp.) 24. 55, 57, 61 (3); ZPGl. 40. 8.

ašaonąm N. 31 (2), 48, 52; Pars. p. 535; Phl. Vd. 19. 25; SlS. 13. 8; Vij. p. 126, 139, 156, 165; W. 1. 2; 7. 2; Yt. 22. 37; Yt. (APZ.) 23. 8; Yt. (Vtp.) 24. 5, 14 (3).

ašaonyāi Yt. 22. 18; Yt. (Vtp.) 24. 64.

ašaonyå Vij. p. 89.

ašaom Yt. (Vtp.) 24. 53.

aša-čiθra Vij. p. 89; W. Yt. 21. 3.

aša-čiθranąm T. 93; W. Yt. 21. 1.

aša-pāntəm [ča Yt. (Vtp.) 24. 42.

ašamāṯ T. 7.

ašaya N. 20, 21, 28 (3), 46 (2), 52; Vij. p. 74; Yt. (Vtp.) 24. 23 (2).

ašayata Yt. (Vtp.) 24. 11.

ašayā N. 15.

ašayå T. 100; ZPGl. 10. 6.

ašayąm T. 25.

ašava N. 47, 60, 89; Phl. Vd. 5. 9; T. 23, 41, 64, 98; Vij. p. 181; Yt. 22. 1, 16; Yt. (APZ.) 23. 4; Yt. (Vtp.) 24. 2, 10, 62.

ašavabyō T. 109.

ašavana N. 47; Phl. Vd. 7. 52.

ašavanəm N. 11, 52, 61, 84;
T. 12, 38, 43, 107; W. 2.
2; 5. 2; Yt. 22. 13; Yt.
(Vtp.) 24. 15, 41, 59. Cf. *an*°.
ašavanō Phl. Ys. 64. 55 (Sp.);
SkN. p. 480; Vij. p. 126;
W. 1. 2; ZPGl. 38. 7.
ašavazaṅhō N. 46.
ašasara N. 67 (3).
ašahe HtN. p. 484; N 47
(6), 49 (2), 61 ; Pars. p. 534,
540 ; Phl. Vd. 8. 72; 9. 27,
28 (5); T. 15, 18, 98, 99,
106; Vij. p. 191; VS. Extr. 4
(2); W. 2. 2 ; Yt. (Vtp.) 24.
15, 18 (2), 42 ; ZPGl. 14. 1.
ašahe [*ča* Pars. p. 534.
ašahē Phl. Ys. 22. 5.
ašahyā N. 34.
aša-xᵛāθrahe N. 65.
ašā T. 31 (2) (for *ašā* *a*ṯ[*ča*
read with D. *ašāaṯ*[*ča*.); Yt.
(Vtp.) 24. 15 ; ZPGl. 12. 11.
ašāi N. 1, 39, 109; Phl. Vd.
19. 18 ; T. 72.
ašāunō Dk. (P. Sj.) 3. 131.
ašāunąm N. 31 (3), 47, 61,
(2); Yt. 22. 39.
ašāunąm [*ča* N. 70.
ašāum Phl. Vd. 18. 2 ; Vij. p.
53; VS. Extr. 4 (2); W. Yt.
21. 1, 7, 9, 11, 13, 15, 17;
Yt. 22. 1, 16 (2), 19, 20, 25 ;
Yt. (Vtp.) 24. 11, 45 (2), 62.
ašā [*ča* W. 1. 1.
ašātōiš Yt. 22. 20.

ašāṯ N. 46 (2), 60, 67, 102 (2);
T. 114.
ašāṯ [*čiṯ* Vij. p. 152.
ašibya ZPGl. 23. 11.
ašivā̊ Phl. Ys. 64 end (Sp.).
ašiš FD. 7; N. 68; Yt. (Vtp.)
24. 8.
ašīm CB.; Yt. (APZ.) 23. 6;
Yt. (Vtp.) 24. 14, 40.
ašənti cf. *frāš*°.
ašəm Dāṯ. 79. 7; N. 6, 20, 35,
39, 46 (2), 84 ; Pars. p. 521,
531, 540; Phl. Vd. 2. 19;
8. 107 ; 19. 18 ; Phl. Ys. 59
end (Sp.); T. 29, 42, 61, 92,
109, 110; Vij. p. 79, 89, 148,
151 (2), 165, 177 ; W. 2. 3;
W. Yt. 21. 2, 3, 7, 9, 11, 13,
15; Yt. (APZ.) 23. 8; Yt.
(Vtp.) 24. 15. Cf. *vīduš*°.
ašəm [*ča* N. 68.
ašəm [*čā* ZPGl. 13. 6.
ašəm-mərənčo Yt. (Vtp.) 24. 2.
ašəm vohu N. 28, 65, 67.
ašəm vohū Dāṯ. 79. 7 ; Dk. 9.
3. 1 ; FD. 7 ; N. 20, 28,
37, 39, 46, 47 (3), 48, 58,
61 (7), 109 ; PI (5) ; Phl. Vd.
9. 32 ; 17. 7, 9 ; 19. 18, 47 ;
SlS. 12. 32 ; T. 113 ; W.
Yt. 21. 11 (Haug.), 13 ; Yt.
(Vtp.) 24. 5, 12, 22, 23, 33,
39, 44, 52, 65.
ašəm vōhū N. 14, 20 (3), 28,
46 (11); Phl. Ys. at ends of
chapters 27 (2). 30. 31. 32.

33. 34. 42. 43. 45. 46. 47.
48. 49. 53. 59. 61. 64. 67.
and 41. 17 and 58. 12 ; Vij.
p. 98, 151, 153, 154 (2), 162,
164 (2), 165.
ašō Phl. Vd. 17. 9.
ašōiš N. 47.
ašō-čiθra W. Yt. 21. 16.
ašō-čiθraēšu T. 56.
ašō-ṯkaēšahe T. 100.
ašō-stūitanąm W. Yt. 21. 10,
12.
ašō-stūitiš W. Yt. 21. 5, 6, 8,
10, 12, 14, 16.
ašō-stūtanąm W. Yt. 21. 6, 8.
aškarᵊ Phl. Vd. 1. 3.
aškāmō Vd. 20. 1 (Geldner ap.
crit.) ; Vij. p. 53.
ašta ZPGl. 12, 2.
aštaᵑhum ZPGl. 1. 9.
aštahmō T. 104.   Cf. tahmō.
aštāitīm AG. 9.
ašti N. 66.
aštiš ZPGl. 12. 9.
aštᵊm N. 105 (3).
aštō-manō Vij. p. 191.
aštraya T. 8.
ašnavāṯ T. 35.
ašnōtᵊmāi N. 70.
ašya Vij. p. 68, 139.
ašy[a]he N. 61.
ašyehe N. 61. v. l. ašayehe ; Vij.
p. 157.
ašyō Phl. Vd. 18. 14 ; Vij. p.
139.
aš-varᵊčå Yt. (APZ.) 23. 2.

azaiti T. 8.
azayanąm cf. an°.
azarᵊm N. 92.
azarᵊmya W. 1. 1.
azarᵊsō Yt. (Vtp.) 24. 45 ;
ZPGl. 11. 12.
azāiti N. 42.
azāθā N. 70.
azāyēš[ča N. 57 (v. l. azy-
āis[ča.)
azinąm ZPGl. 12. 2.
azīš Phl. Ys. 38. 13 (Sp.).
azᵊm N. 46 ; T. 58, 82 ; Vij. p.
126, 138 ; Vth. 14 ; W. 4. 2 ;
Yt. 22. 11; Yt. 24. 20 (2),
21, 46, 49, 58 ; ZPGl. 12. 2.
azō N. 58.
azdāi N. 83.
azyāiš N. 57 (2).
azyå N. 85.
azrazdāi N. 17.
[aža] v. l. Phl. Ys. 64. 48 (Sp.),
cf. Geldner Avesta on Ys. 65.
12.
ažiš A. 78.
ažōiš N. 48 ; Yt. (APZ.) 23. 3.
aha Phl. Ys. 64. 48.
ahaową (?) N. 83.
ahaxtō N. 6.
[ahasrīma] v. l. Phl. Ys. 64.
48 (Sp.).
ahi N. 10 ; Yt. 22. 10 ; Yt.
(Vtp.) 24. 22, 57.
ahuirᵊm Pars. p. 531.
ahubya ZPGl. 13. 12.
ahuna N. 103.

ahunanąm vairyanąm N. 102

ahunavaṭ N. 72.

ahunavaṭ[ča N. 46.

ahunahe T. 54.

ahunāṭ vairyāṭ N. 68.

ahunəm vairīm N. 20, 81 ; Pars.
p. 531 ; Vij. p. 67.

ahunō vairyō Phl. Vd. 2. 10 ;
W. Yt. 21. 4.

ahunąs[ča N. 50.

ahunvitīm Vij. p. 139.

ahumaiti T. 57 (read *humaiti*).

ahura T. 29 ; Vij. p. 12, 50.

ahura mazda N. 46 ; Vij. p. 99 ;
W. Yt. 21. 1 ; Yt. 22. 1, 20 ;
Yt. (Vtp.) 24. 20, 24, 65.

ahuradātahe W. 5. 1.

ahuradātəm W. 5. 2 ; Yt. (APZ.)
23. 7.

ahurahe CB ; N. 46, 48 (3),
58 ; Pars. p. 521 ; SlS. 13.
8 ; Vij. p. 165 (2) ; W. 7. 1
(2) ; Yt. (Vtp.) 24. 26, 46.

ahurahe mazdå N. 28, 31 (5),
37 (2), 46 (5), 47 (5), 49 (2)
58, 61 (3), 65 ; Pars. p. 535 ;
SkN. p. 480 ; T. 23, 32, 88
(2), 92 ; Vij. p. 79 (2), 99,
126, 138, 141, 153, 159, 162,
164 (2) ; Vth. 1, 6 ; W. 5.
1 ; Yt. 22. 13, 38 (3) ; Yt.
(Vtp.) 24. 20, 21, 33, 40 ;
ZPGl. 38. 6.

ahurahyā Phl. Ys. 38. 8 (Sp.).

ahurā N. 46 ; Phl. Vd. 19. 10 ;
T. 28.

ahurāi N. 28 ; SlS. 13. 9 ; W.
9. 2.

ahurāi mazdāi N. 46 (3) ; Phl.
Vd. 19. 25 ; Vij. p. 181 ; Yt.
(Vtp.) 24. 33 (2), 51.

ahurānīš Phl. Ys. 38. 8 (Sp.).

ahurāne N. 46 (2), 48 (2) ; Vij.
p. 165 ; W. 7. 1, 2.

ahurəm[ča mazdąm Yt. (Vtp.)
24. 14.

ahurəm mazdąm N. 61, 65, 70,
103 ; Pars. p. 534 ; Phl. Ys.
9. 27 ; T. 22 ; Vij. p. 52 (2),
54, 128 (2) ; W. 5. 2 ; W.
Yt. 21. 1. 3 ; Yt. 22. 1, 14 ;
Yt. (Vtp.) 24. 60.

ahurō Phl. Ys. 67 end (Sp.) ;
Vij. p. 50 ; Yt. 22. 2 ; Yt.
(Vtp.) 24. 53.

ahurō mazdå A. 57, 81 ; Phl.
Vd. 2. 32 ; T. 55, 58, 82 ;
Vij. p. 50, 51 (2), 54, 152,
180, 181 ; Vth. 14 ; W. 4.
2 ; W. Yt. 21. 2, 7, 9, 11,
13, 15, 17 ; Yt. 22. 2, 4, 6,
17, 20, 40 ; Yt. (Vtp.) 24.
11, 24, 39, 54, 63 ; ZPGl.
13. 3 ; 16. 11.

ahurå Pars. p. 540 (read °*rā*).

ahū Dk. 8. 46. 2 ; N. 36 ; Pars.
p. 531 ; Pl. (8) ; Phl. Vd.
19. 2, 10, 22 ; Phl. Ys. at
ends of 28. 29. 30. 31. 32. 33.
34. 43. 50. 59. 60. 62. 70. and
at 41. 17 ; 58. 12 and 67. 41.
Cf. also *yaθā ahū vairyō*.

ahūiryehe N. 61

ahūm Phl. Ys. 27 end ; T. 43, 83, 91 ; Yt. 22. 16 (2), 34 (2); Yt. (APZ.) 23. 8 ; Yt. (Vtp.) 24. 5, 62 (2).

ahūm [*ča* Pars. p. 534.

ahūmbiš Pars. p. 540.

ahūrāne N. 109.

ahū vairyō Dk. 7. 4. 41 ; N. 37 (4), 46 (4) ; Phl. Vd. 9. 27 ; 19. 2, 22 ; Phl. Ys. 28 end ; 29 end ; W. 6. 1 (3) ; 7. 9 (2) ; Yt. (APZ.) 23. 8. Cf. *yaθā ahū vairyō*.

ahe N. 22 ; T. 33 ; Vij. p. 184 ; W. 4. 2 ; Yt. 22. 37 ; Yt. (Vtp.) 24. 25.

ahe [*ča* N. 48 ; Yt. (Vtp.) 24. 32.

ahąxštaγnāi Yt. (Vtp.) 24. 19.

ahąxštotəmō-ahąxšta Yt. (Vtp.) 24. 19.

ahma N. 103 (read *hama*).

ahmat̰ T. 39 ; Vth. 4, 9, 11.

ahmāi N. 34, 39, 103, 109 ; PI ; Pars. p. 535, 540 ; Phl. Vd.

19. 18 ; Phl. Ys. 42 end ; 44 end ; 45 end ; W. 2 ; Yt. 22. 2 ; Yt. (APZ.) 23. 8 ; Yt. (Vtp.) 24. 31, 34, 37, 38 (2), 46 (2), 54 ; ZPGl. 20. 7.

ahmākəm W. 1. 2 ; Yt. (Vtp.) 24. 47 ; ZPGl. 20. 7.

ahmākəm [*ča* CB.

ahmāt̰ CB (2) ; Dk. (P.Sj.) 3. 131 ; N. 15, 18, 42, 43, 48 ; Phl. Vd. 4. 10 ; T. 66, 105 ; Vij. p. 89 ; Yt. (Vtp.) 24. 12.

ahmi N. 8, 61 ; Phl. Vd. 2. 5 ; 8. 74 ; T. 22, 48, 58 ; Vij. p. 5, 12, 50 ; Yt. 22. 11 ; Yt. (APZ.) 23. 1 ; Yt. (Vtp.) 24. 1. 58.

ahmī N. 103 ; T. 22.

ahme N. 8.

ahmyā CB. (6) ; Yt. (Vtp.) 24. 48 (3).

ahyā Dk. 8. 46. 2 ; N. 23 (2), 34. At end of Phl. Ys. 28. 30. 31. 32. 33 and 34.

ahvāstāiš [*ča* N. 57.

a.

ā Ep. M. 1. 4. 3 ; N. 2, 8, 36, 42, 43, 48, 50, 65, 77, 82, 96 ; Phl. Vd. 3. 14 ; Phl. Ys. 27 end ; T. 43 (2) ; Vij. p. 89, 146 ; W. 8. 1 ; 9. 2 ; W. Yt. 21. 4 ; Yt. (Vtp.) 24. 18 (3) ; ZPGl. 12. 10 ; 20. 6, 8. Cf. *ādim*.

āat̰ A. 25, 26, 27, 57, 81 ; N. 9, 10 (2), 13, 14, 26 (2), 34, 38, 39, 46, 47, 53, 55, 60, 62, 66 (2), 67, 72, 73, 74, 75, 76, 83, 88, 90, 95, 96, 97, 100, 101, 102, 103 (3), 104, 105 ; Phl. Vd. 1. 1 ; 2. 32 ; 5. 9 ; T. 78, 80, 81 ; Vij. p. 23, 24

(2), 126, 134, 136, 138, 145
(2), 148, 158, 179 (2), 180,
184, Vth. 6, 19 ; W. 3.
2 ; Yt. 22. 2, 4, 6, 8, 10,
11, 13, 14 (2), 17, 20, 26,
41, 42 ; Yt. (APZ.) 23. 1 ;
Yt. (Vtp.) 24. 8, 13, 22,
24, 31 (2), 33, 41 (2), 43,
49 (2), 54, 55, 58, 60 (2),
62 ; ZPGl. 12. 5 ; 20. 7.
āi Phl. Vd. 18. 2 ; Yt. (Vtp.)
24. 11.
āiti N. 2 (3) ; Yt. (Vtp.) 24. 36.
Cf. *par°*.
āite T. 68.
āiθavantəm Yt. 22. 17.
ākačiθamanąm N. 63.
ākå N. 6, 63.
*āxšti to be read for *āhišti* in
T. 50.
āg[a]va N. 54.
āčikatōiš[ča Yt. (Vtp.) 24. 10.
ājaɣaurva N. 54.
ājasaiti A. 51.
ātarə N. 65 ; Phl. Vd. 7. 52 (2).
ātarə-kərəta ZPGl. 21. 5.
ātarə-taraēnaēmāṯ ZPGl. 21. 5.
ātarə-friθitəm[ča ZPGl. 21. 7.
ātarəbyō N. 47 (3).
ātarə-marəzanō ZPGl. 21. 6.
ātarəvaxšahe Yt. (Vtp.) 24. 15.
ātarə-vaxšō ZPGl. 21. 4. Cf.
ātɣa°.
ātarə-vazanō ZPGl. 21. 4.
ātarəm Ep. M. 1. 4. 3 ; Phl.
Vd. 3. 14 ; Yt. (APZ.) 23. 6.

ātarəm[ča N. 68 ; Yt. 22. 13 ;
Yt. (Vtp.) 24. 40.
ātarō Yt. (Vtp.) 24. 26.
ātarš N. 37, 46 (2), 103 (2) ;
Vij. p. 79, 133 ; SkN. p. 480 ;
T. 23, 32 ; Yt. (Vtp.) 24.
38 ; ZPGl. 38. 5.
ā-tāpayeiti Ep. M. 1. 4. 3 (v. l.
ātāpayaēta).
ātarəbyō N. 65.
ātəe FD. 7.
ātraēibyō Vij. p. 126.
ātravaxšahe N. 73, 79, 81.
ātravaxšō N. 37 (2). Cf. *ātarə°*
ātrəm[ča N. 73, 81.
āθa ZPGl. 20. 9.
āθaiti W. 8. 2.
āθwyānəm W. 2. 2.
āθwyānō W. 2. 1, 3.
āθwyānōiš Yt. (APZ.) 23. 4 ;
Yt. (Vtp.) 24. 2.
āθra N. 11.
āθraiąm FD. 5 ; SlS. 13. 17.
āθraē[ča N. 74.
āθrava Yt. (Vtp.) 24. 9.
āθravaxšəm N. 82.
āθravana N. 3 ; Vij. p. 138.
āθravanō N. 86.
āθras[ča N. 49 (2), 73, 74 ;
Pars. p. 540 ; T. 88.
āθrətīm N. 46.
āθrəm Yt. (Vtp.) 24. 4.
āθrō Dāṯ. 43. 2, 5 ; N. 37, 46,
47 (4), 65, 70 (2), 75, 79
(2) ; Vij. p. 99, 134, 141 ; Yt.
22. 41 ; Yt. (Vtp.) 24. 51.

āθrąm [ča Vij. p. 89.

āθrnəntəm N. 2.

ādarə FD. 3.

ādarəyēite T. 123.

adāi N. 46 (2).

ādāta ZPGl. 20. 10.

ādāṭ T. 5.

ādim Vth. 1 ; Yt. 22. 7, 16, 25, 34 ; Yt. (Vtp.) 24. 55, 57.

ādərəzayōiṭ N. 3.

[ādå] v. l. N. 6.

āδa N. 22, 32, (2).

āδairi N. 85.

āδayōiṭ N. 83.

āṭ N. 14, 28 ; T. 29 ; ZPGl. 20. 8.

āpa N. 66 ; Yt. (Vtp.) 24. 8.

āpəm FD. 7 ; N. 70, 77 ; Vij. p. 5 ; W. Yt. 21. 3 ; ZPGl. 16. 5 ; 17. 3.

āpe N. 28, 48, 67, 69.

āpō N. 69, 108 ; W. 1. 2.

āfeš N. 69 (read āfš).

[āfraōxte] v. l. N. 13.

āfritiš T. 65.

āfritōiṭ SIS. 13. 43.

āfritōiš N. 61.

āfrin [əm] Yt. (Vtp.) 24. 3.

āfrimari N. 12.

āfrimnō N. 12.

āfrivanaēibiš W. 8. 1.

āfrītīm T. 66.

āfrīnāṭ Yt. (Vtp.) 24. 38.

āfrīnāmi A. 111 ; AG. 10 ; N. 47 (2), 69 ; Vij, p. 164 ; Yt. (APZ.) 23. 1, 8 ; ZPGl. 17. 5.

āfrīnənti Vij. p. 96.

āfrīnəntu CB.

āfrīnəm Yt. (APZ.) 23. 2, 8.

āfrī-vačå Yt. (APZ.) 23. 1 ; Yt. (Vtp.) 24. 1.

ābərətəm ZPGl. 21. 8.

ābərətō Yt. (Vtp.) 24. 15.

ā-bərəs N. 77.

ānəm FD. 7.

āmaēiδyāṭ N. 46.

āmāta ZPGl. 19. 9.

āmiθnāiti A. 53.

āmravī W. 9. 2.

āmruye Yt. (Vtp.) 24. 39.

āmrūta cf. čaθruš°, θriš° and biš°.

āyapta Yt. (Vtp.) 24. 25.

āyaptəm Yt. (Vtp.) 24. 38, 46.

āyātəmnahe N. 28.

āyēse Vij. p. 141.

āraočayeiti Phl. Vd. 2. 40.

ā-rəitīm [ča T. 87.

ārəšvā cf. uz°.

ārōima Yt. (Vtp.) 24. 38.

ārmaitiš Pars. p. 541 ; Phl. Vd. 9. 12 (2), 32 ; Vij. p. 156 ; ZPGl. 13. 1.

ārmaitiš [ča Pars. p. 541.

ārmaitī Phl. Ys. 67 end (Sp.).

ārmaitīm Pars. p. 534 ; Yt. (Vtp.) 24. 50.

ārmaite T. 51.

ārmaēštaya N. 67.

ārmata ZPGl. 21. 8.

ārmitōiš Vij. p. 184.

ārmutō N. 24.

āva N. 16.
āvaṇhe N. 70.
āvayanti N. 31.
āvayantī N. 61.
āviš T. 76.
āviš[ča T. 75.
āvoya N. 84 (2), v. l. *āvōya.*
āvōya Yt. (Vtp.) 24. 43.
ās T. 105 ; ZPGl. 20. 5.
āsa N. 4.
āsāṯ N. 19.
āsu ZPGl. 20. 5.
āsuyā[ča W. 8. 1.
āstaya N. 65.
āstayeiti N. 82.
āstarayeiti N. 12.
āstāθa N. 2.
āstāyā N. 46.
āstāraiti N. 109 ; Yt. (Vtp.) 24. 37.
āstārayaiti Vth. 11.
āstārayeiti T. 12.
āstārayeite N. 12.
āsti Vij. p. 181.
āstuye SlS. 13. 1.
āstūitiš N. 103.
āste ZPGl. 20. 6.
āstravanəm cf. *an°*

āstrāinti N. 9.
āstryačite T. 121, 122.
āstryanti N. 4.
āstryeiti N. 11, 13, 14, 15, 18 (2), 30, 42, 44.
āstryeite N. 14, 15, 22.
āstryenti N. 10. (v. l. *astryeite*).
āsnatāra N. 75.
āsnatārəm N. 82; ZPGl. 21. 8.
āsnatārš N. 79.
āsnayāṯ N. 75.
āsnāθraṯ N. 80.
āsnāθrō Yt. (Vtp.) 24. 15.
āsnąm N. 4.
āzaiti N. 43.
āzaintivaitiš ZPGl. 8. 6.
āzǣiti N. 69 (2), 83, 109.
āzātayǟ Yt. 22. 9; Yt. (Vtp.) 24. 56.
āzārayōiš HtN. p. 483.
āzī N. 67; T. 5.
āzīzušte T. 96.
āzōiš ZPGl. 20. 9.
āhi N. 10 (v l. *ahi*).
āhišti T. 50 (read *āxšti*).
āhuirīm AG. 10.
āhurahe N. 70.
āhe N. 10.

i.

iti N. 4.
itəm cf. *aiw°.*
iθa N. 47, 50, 67, 101.
iθā Daṯ 79. 1, 2, 3, 4, 7 (2), 8; N. 14, 28 (4).
iθyejaṇuhaiti A. 25, 26, 27, 28.
iθyejaṇuhataṯ Yt. 22. 16, 34.
iθyejaṇh- cf. *aiθ°.*
iθyejaṇhataṯ Yt. (Vtp.) 24. 62.
iθra N. 85 ; T. 45, 90 ; Yt. 22. 39. (Cf. also *iθrišūm?*)

[*iθrapaitiš*] v. l. FD. 4 (for
  aēθ°).
iθrišūm N. 65, v. l. *iθra išūm.*
iδa Vij. p. 156; Yt. (Vtp.) 24.
  13, 36 (2), 46, 49 (2).
iṯ Yt. 22. 10 ; Yt. (Vtp.) 24. 57.
imaṯ N. 46 (2) ; W. Yt. 21. 14,
  16; Yt. 22. 2, 20; Yt. (Vtp.)
  24. 9 (2), 20 (2), 21.
imā T. 29.
iməm N. 46 (2).
imå̄ N. 47.
imąm N. 46, 71.
imąm[*ča* W. Yt. 21. 16.
irite cf. *paiti°*.
iriθy- cf. *pairi°* and *para°*.
iriθyāṯ Vij. p. 23 ; Yt. (Vtp.) 24.
  44.
irisatanąm Vij. p. 138.
irista Vij. p. 24, 25, 158 ; W.
  4. 3. Cf. *para°*.
iristatanūm Vij. p. 139.
iristanąm Vij. p. 146, 156 ; Yt.
  22. 39.
irišantinąm N. 2.
[*irišintanam*] v l N ?
irišintō Yt. (Vtp.) 24. 44.
irišintąm Yt. (Vtp.) 24. 44.
irišta N. 56.
irīraiθyāṯ Vij. p. 157.
irīritānahe T. 44.
irīriθāne T. 74.
irīriθušō Phl. Vd. 3. 40.

iṯ T. 27 (2).
īm ZPGl. 12. 7.
iš T. 6.

irīrīš N. 95.
ivərbarəs[*ča* N. 99.
isaiti A. 48.
isaēta T. 39.
[*i*] *saṯ-vāstrahe* N. 31 (to be read
  for *saṯ-vāstrahe*)
isāi ZPGl. 14. 8.
isāṯ N. 109 (2). Cf. *upō*.
isənti A. 41.
isəmnō N. 52, 53.
isōiṯ N. 12, 109. Cf. *upaōisāṯ*
  and *upō°*.
isti A. 82 (3) ; T. 12.
iste T. 12.
iš N. 26.
išaiti Yt. 22. 2, 20.
išaēta Yt. (Vtp.) 24. 12.
išaṯ Phl. Vd. 2. 32.
išantəm cf. *paitišantəm.*
išars(*-pasča*) Vij. p. 138.
išarə-štāitya Phl. Vd. 7. 72.
išīm W. 4. 1 (2).
išum cf. *asta°.*
išūm T. 34. (cf. *iθrišūm* ?).
iš[*ča* N. 109 (2).
ištaēšna N 58
ištōiš Yt. (Vtp.) 24. 46.
išyāmahe cf. *fraēš°.*
išyō Phl. Ys. 27 end.
izyati[*ča* Yt. (Vtp.) 24. 30.
izyeiti Yt. (Vtp.) 24. 29.
izā[*čā* Pars. p. 541 (*°čå̄*) ; Phl.
  Vd. 9. 12 (2), 32.

ī.

īžayå̄ N. 70.
īžā[*ča* Vij. p. 156.
īžəm N. 34.

u.

u N. 42, 44, 61, 103 ; Phl. Vd.
7. 52 (2).

uiti N. 37 ; Yt. 22. 42 (2) ;
Yt. (Vtp.) 24. 11, 43.

uiθe N. 61.

uxta cf. *duž*°.

uxtā T. 55.

[*n*]*uxturušu* N. 68. (The Bombay edition has *nux*°.)

uxδa Phl. Vd. 2. 10.

uxδanąm[*ča* Vij. p. 25.

uxδa-vačaṅhō Yt. (Vtp.) 24. 17.

uxδašna ZPGl. 9. 5.

uxδahyā[*čā* T. 70.

uxδā T. 29.

uxδəm Vij. p. 24 ; W. 9. 1 ;
Yt. (Vtp.) 24. 20, 22, 26, 28,
53 ; ZPGl. 9. 3.

uxδō Phl. Vd. 8. 8 ; W. 9. 1.

uxδō-vačastəmō T. 47.

uxδō-vačąm T. 47.

uxδā̊ ZPGl. 9. 2.

uxδąm ZPGl. 32. 6.

uxšayeiti N. 32.

uxšyā N. 47.

uγrāi N. 61.

uγrəm Yt. (APZ.) 23. 3 ; ZPGl.
24. 2.

ujuštānəm Vij. p. 179.

uta A. 82 (2) ; Yt. (APZ) 23.
2 ; ZPGl. 23. 10.

utā ZPGl. 12. 5.

uθahe N. 65.

uθahe[*ča* N. 65.

uθəm N. 65.

[*uθδahe*] v. l. N. 65.

upa N. 17, 20, 21 (4), 28, 53,
58, 68, 71, 79 (3), 101 (2),
103, 109 (2); T. 61, 71, 110;
Vij. p. 25, 137, 139, 179 (*up*);
Yt. 22. 2, 4, 20; Yt. (Vtp.)
24. 13, 22, 23, 38.

upaiti Phl. Vd. 3. 14. (v. l.
upaēta.)

upairi T. 78; VS. Extr. 1, 2, 3, 4.

upaδisāt̰ N. 11. Cf. *upōis*°.

upa-θwərəsōit̰ N. 105.

upa-θrəstəm[*čat̰* N. 51 (D.).
(Bombay edition reads *apa*°.)

upabarāt̰ Yt. (Vtp.) 24. 38.

upabarō N. 108.

upa-bərətayaē[*ča* N. 45.

upaṅharəzaiti Vij. p. 179.

upaṅharəzāt̰ Vij. p. 179.

upamanāi N. 61.

upamanąm N. 105 (2).

upa-manyən Vij. p. 137.

upayat̰ N. 12.

uparatātəm W. 5. 2.

uparatātō W. 5. 1.

uparasmanāi N. 92.

uparāt̰ N. 93; T. 38.

upariharəštəe N. 108.

uparō ZPGl. 9. 12.

uparō-kairīm W. 4. 1.

uparō-kairyehe N. 47; Yt. (Vtp.)
24. 24.

upa-vāvō Yt. 22. 7, 25.

upasu N. 109.

upa-staoiti Yt. (Vtp.) 24. 39.

upa-stuitīm Yt. (Vtp.) **24**. 29.

upasraotārō N. 38, 39 (3).

upazbaya Yt. (Vtp.) **24**. 43.

upa-zbayata Yt. (Vtp.) **24**. 38, 39.

upā Yt. (Vtp.) **24**. 27, 45.

upā[*ča* Yt. **22**. 6.

upəma N. 90.

upəməm[*ča* Vij. p. 128.

upō N. 53, 109. Cf. *isāṯ*.

upōisaiti N. 109. Cf. *upaōi°*.

upōisōiṯ N. 11 (3).

ubōibyā ZPGl. 2. 11. *uboya* R.

ubjāitē Phl. Vd. 7. ʼ52.

ubdaēna ZPGl. 24. 1.

una ZPGl. 23. 9.

unəm ZPGl. 24. 2.

unąm N. 100.

uməm[*čiṯ* N. 103.

uravar̆ā N. 101. Cf. *urv°*.

uru N. 91.

urua ZPGl. 7. 13.

uruθaṯ ZPGl. 24. 2.

uruθwarə ZPGl. 10. 7.

uruθmyanąm Yt. (Vtp.) **24**. 22.

uruδiδieiti ZPGl. 24. 1.

urupa Yt. (APZ.) **23**. 2.

uruna A. 48.

urunaē[*ča* ZPGl. 11. 10.

uruna[*ča* W. Yt. **21**. 4.

urunas[*ča* N. 70.

urune FD. 3 ; N. 52, 67 (2); T. 83, 101 ; W. **6**. 1 (6); Yt. (Vtp.) **24**. 32.

urunō N. 84.

urusta Yt. (Vtp.) **24**. 22.

urusvaišitiš cf. *pairi°*.

urušnōiš FD. 7.

urūtaṭahe Yt. (Vtp.) **24**. 47.

urva N. 84; T.18, 79; Vij. p. 116; Yt. **22**. 1, 2, 3, 5, 7, 8, 10, 15 (4), 19, 20, 25, 26, 29–33 ; Yt. (Vtp.) **24**. 42, 53, 54, 55, 57, 61 (3); ZPGl. 23. 9.

urvaixti cf. *fra°*.

urvaitim cf. *avačō°* and *vačō°*.

urvaitya N. 54.

urvaire Phl. Vd. **19**. 18 ; Yt. (Vtp.) **24**. 22.

urvaēdąs ZPGl. 24. 1.

urvaēsa ZPGl. 23. 9. Cf. *daṇhā°*.

urvaēsayāṯ T. 35.

urvaēsāṯ Yt. (Vtp.) **24**. 29.

urvaēsəm Yt. (Vtp.) **24**. 29.

urvaēse N. 47 ; W. Yt. **21**. 15.

urvaēsō ZPGl. 23. 8.

urvatəm ZPGl. 10. 11.

urvaθa° cf. *aurvaθanąm*.

urvaθō Yt. (APZ.) **23**. 4 ; ZPGl. 23. 8.

urvara N. 28, 90. Cf. *urav°*.

urvaranąm Phl. Vd. **5**. 19 ; Yt. (Vtp.) **24**. 22.

urvarayå N. 90, 100.

urvarāhu[*ča* Yt. **22**. 7 ; Yt. (Vtp.) **24**. 55.

urvarō-strayąs[*ča* Yt. **22**. 13.

urvarō-strąm[*ča* Yt. (Vtp.) **24**. 37, 59.

urvar̆ā W. **1**. 2 ; W. Yt. **21**. 3.

urvarās̆[*čā* T. 115.

urvarąm N. 98.

urvāxšahe Yt. (APZ.) 23. 3.

urvānəm T. 44, 74. Vij. p. 25, 157. Cf. *vahištō°*.

urvānəm [*ča* T. 71.

urvānō Phl. Vd. 19. 30 ; Vij. p. 156.

urvāsnyå Vij. p. 158.

urvāsma T. 82.

urvāsmana Yt. (Vtp.) 24. 50.

urviṭyeiti T. 119.

urvis- cf. *fraoirišaiti* and *vī°*.

urvištrəm Yt. 22. 17, 35.

urvīštrəm Yt. (Vtp.) 24. 63.

urvąni FD. 3.

urvąnō A. 3 ;. Yt. 22. 39. Cf *vahištō°*.

uva ZPGl. 23. 10.

us N. 46 (2), 48 ; Vij. p. 99 ; W. 4. 3; 7. 2 ; Yt. (Vtp.) 24. 50 ; ZPGl. 9. 12 ; 23. 8, 9.

usa Yt. (APZ.) 23. 2.

usaiti N. 6 (2) ; Yt. (Vtp.) 24. 34. Cf. *an°* and *vi°*

usas [*ča* Yt. (Vtp.) 24. 34, 46.

usən Yt. (Vtp.) 24. 42.

usəhištaṭ A. 12 ; Phl. Vd. 2. 10.

us [*ča* N. 67 ; Phl. Vd. 2. 40 ; Yt. (Vtp.) 24. 46.

usjasaiti N. 68.

us-jiti Yt. (APZ.) 23. 1 ; Yt. (Vtp.) 24. 1.

ustānazastō N. 23.

ustəme W. Yt. 21. 15.

ustryamnō W. Yt. 21. 11.

usbī(*barāmi*) Vij. p. 166.

usmahi [*ča* A. 1.

usyō T. 121.

usyąstačō A. 60.

usraočayeiti Phl. Vd. 2. 40.

usrārayå Yt. (Vtp.) 24. 41.

uszayånte Yt. (APZ.) 23. 1.

uš ZPGl. 23. 11.

ušaðąm ZPGl. 10. 8.

ušaŋhąm Yt. 22. 41.

ušastara Phl. Vd. 1. 18.

ušahinanąm N. 46.

uši Yt. 22. 38.

uši-daranəm Yt. 22. 38.

uši-darənahe N. 65.

uši-dąm Yt. 22. 38.

ušibyō N. 26.

ušąm(*-surąm*) ZPGl. 42. 10.

ušta Yt. 22. 16 ; Yt. (Vtp.) 24. 30, 53 (2), 62 ; ZPGl. 23. 10.

uštatāite Yt. (Vtp.) 24. 33.

uštatātəm Yt. 22. 2 ; Yt. (Vtp.) ·24. 54 ; ZPGl. 23. 11.

uštatās T. 84.

ušta-bərəitīm [*ča* T. 88.

ušta-bərətis [*ča* N. 48.

uštanavaitīš T. 123.

uštanəm Pars. p. 521.

uštanå cf. *uz°*.

uštavaitīm N. 46 ; Yt. 22. 2 ; Yt. (Vtp.) 24. 54.

uštavaityå N. 102 (2).

uštavaētayå N. 102.

uštā N. 34, 39 (2), 109 (2) ; Phl. Vd. 19. 18 (2) ; Phl. Ys. 42 end. 44 end. 45 end ; Yt. 22. 2 (2) ; Yt. (Vtp.) 24. 54 (2).

uštāna Vth. 10.

uštāna [*ča* T. 35.

uštrahe T. 65.

ušra N. 103.

uzayairanąm N. 50 (v. l. °*rinąm*).

uzayarāi N. 47, 49.

uzayarna Vij. p. 157.

uzayeirine N. 9.

uzarɘnō T. 117.

uzarɘm N. 47.

uzaryarāṯ N. 50.

uzas [*ča* ZPGl. 17. 5.

uzašta ZPGl. 41. 2.

uzāiti ZPGl. 13. 2.

uzārɘšvā N. 46.

uzuštanå T. 123.

uzōiš Phl. Vd. 1. 15.

uzgɘrɘptɘm Vij. p. 128.

uzgɘrɘsnāvayō N. 94.

uzgɘrɘmbyō Yt. 22. 8, 26 ; Yt. (Vtp.) 24. 55.

uzgōurvayāṯ Vij. p. 128, 145.

uzjasɘnti Phl. Vd. 1. 15.

uzdanuhu [*čiṯ* N. 9.

uzbarɘnti N. 93.

uzbārayaṯ Yt. (Vtp.) 24. 23, 28.

uzyazdāna ZPGl. 8. 1.

uzyāθramayā Dk. (P.Sj.) 3. 131.

uzyeiti Yt. (Vtp.) 24. 30.

uzyō ZPGl. 23. 10.

uzrātiš T. 116.

uzvarɘštayō Phl. Vd. 7. 52.

uzvarɘzyāṯ Yt. (Vtp.) 24. 26.

ū.

ūθ N. 65 (read *ūθyaṯ* for *ūθ yaṯ*).

ə.

ərɘγatō A. 28.

ərɘγaṯ T. 93.

ərɘčištɘm N. 2 (MS. **TD**. reads *ərɘčništɘm*).

ərɘtō cf. *aiwiᵘ*.

ərɘθō N. 47.

ərɘdrafšuyå Yt. (Vtp.) 24. 56.

ərɘdvafšnyå Yt. 22. 9.

ərɘδaēm ZPGl. 10. 10.

ərɘnāišti T. 91.

ərɘš Phl. Vd. 19. 10.

ərɘzaurvāēsāṯ ZPGl. 42. 8.

ərɘzatɘm A. 84.

ərɘzatō A. 17.

ərɘzi ZPGl. 11. 1.

ərɘzu ZPGl. 10. 4.   Cf. *baē°*.

ərɘzubya N. 65.

ərɘzva N. 83.

ərezvō N. 69, v. l. 79; Phl. **18**. 43 ; W. **4**. 1.

ərɘžuxδō W. Yt. 21. 4.

əvisaēušva N. 16.

əvīsɘmnō T. 121.

o.

oium A. 51 (v. l. *oiuim*); W. Yt. 21. 5 (v. l. *ōium*).

ouye Vij. p. 133.

ō.

[ōium] v. l. W. Yt. 21. 5.
ōiθra ZPGl. 3. 1.
ōim N. 14 ; ZPGl. 1. 4.

ōyum N. 14.
ōyəm N. 42.
ōyąm N. 42.

å.

å̃ṇha T. 59 (cf. nå̃ṇha); ZPGl.
   8. 3.
å̃ṇhanąm Yt. 22. 14 ; Yt. (Vtp.)
   24. 60.
å̃ṇhāδō Yt. (Vtp.) 24. 35, 36.

å̃ṇhāṯ N. 65.
å̃ṇhānō N. 37 ; T. 10.
å̃ṇhō cf. an°.
å̃ṇhąm N. 42.
å̃ntyå ZPGl. 8. 2.

ą.

ąsavō N. 108.
ąsta Yt. (Vtp.) 24. 44.
ąstā N. 41 (2).
ąstəm A. 48.

ązahū Yt. (Vtp.) 24. 51.
ązå N. 67.
ąząs[ča N. 47.

k.

kaityā W. 9. 2.
kaini[ča Yt. (Vtp.) 24. 28.
kaininō Phl. Vd. 12. 4.
kainīnō Yt. 22. 9 ; Yt. (Vtp.)
   24. 56.
kairi- cf. uparō°.
kairim N. 72.
[kaua] v. l. FD. 6.
katār N. 5 (read katārō).
katārəm N. 3.
katārō N. 5, 41.
kaθa N. 33 ; Yt. 22. 16 (3), 34
   (3) ; Yt. (Vtp.) 24. 51, 62 (2).
kaθa[ča N. 37.
kaṯ Dk. 9. 20. 1; N. 2, 6, 16,
   18, 24, 108 ; SlS. 8. 22 ; T.
   54, 69 (2).
kaṯ[čiṯ N. 100.

kaṇhąm N. 37.
kaṅhå̃s[čiṯ W. Yt. 21. 5.
kana Yt. (Vtp.) 24. 21 (2).
kanənti Phl. Vd. 3. 40.
kamərəδāṯ Yt. 22. 20.
kaya N. 34, 35, 36, 54 ; ZPGl.
   6. 12 ; 7. 3.
kayaδəm T. 19.
kayā[čiṯ N. 40.
kara N. 5.
karaiθin N. 97.
karapanō W. 2. 2.
karašō ZPGl. 18. 6.
karahe cf. raēθwiš°.
karətās[ča N. 87.
karətō-dąsuš Yt. 22. 41.
karəna T. 101.
karšas[čiṯ ZPGl. 18. 8.

karšuąm ZPGl. 18. 7.
karšōiṯ N. 48.
karšti Yt. (Vtp.) 24. 33.
karštu Yt. (Vtp.) 24. 28.
karštōe ZPGl. 18. 9.
karšvarə W. Yt. 21. 14.
karšvǎ ZPGl. 18. 9.
kava Yt. (APZ.) 23. 2, 3, 7 ;
   Yt. (Vtp.) 24. 1 (2), 2, 6, 8,
   9, 10, 12, 19, 20, 22, 24, 26,
   28, 34, 37, 40, 42, 45, 53,
   65.
kavaēm Yt. (Vtp.) 24. 40.
kava[čiṯ N. 70; Phl. Vd. 1.
   14; ZPGl. 40. 5.
kavandəm Yt. (Vtp.) 24. 26.
kavahmāṯ Phl. Vd. 3. 42.
kavōiš Yt. (APZ.) 23. 1.
kasištahe Phl. Vd. 18. 43.
kasištəm Dk. (P. Sj.) 3. 131.
kasu-xraθwa N. 40.
kas[čiṯ N. 63 ; ZPGl. 40. 7.
kasyaɴhō ZPGl. 7. 3.
kasvikąmčina Phl. Vd. 4. 1.
kaša Vij. p. 89. Cf. *nasu°*.
kašaibya ZPGl. 10. 7.
kašaēibya N. 85. (v. l. *kašaē-
   bya*.)
kašinąm Vij. p. 146.
kašəm N. 28.
kašǎ ZPGl. 18. 5.
kahmāi[čiṯ Yt. 22. 2 ; Yt.
   (Vtp.) 24. 53, 54 ; ZPGl. 13.
   5.
kahmāṯ N. 46, 47, 48, 49, 50,
   51, 61, 62.

kahmi W. Yt. 21. 1.
kahyāi[čiṯ N. 65.
kahyā[čiṯ N. 46 (2) ; T. 98.
kā A. 17 ; N. 103, 108 ; Phl.
   Ys. 9. 25 ; W. Yt. 21. 6, 8,
   10, 12, 14, 16.
kā[čiṯ N. 109 (2).
kām Yt. 22. 20 ; Yt. (Vtp.) 24.
   65.
kāmō cf. *aš°*.
kārayō[vā Yt. (Vtp.) 24. 13.
kāravaiti Yt. (Vtp.) 24. 49.
kāšayāṯ T. 79.
kinəm cf. *fra°*.
kimąm Yt. 22. 20.
kuirisahe Vij. p. 139.
kuxšnīša N. 48 ; W. 7. 2.
kuxšnūša Vij. p. 165.
kuxšnvānō Yt. (Vtp.) 24. 59.
kuxšnvąnō Yt. 22. 13.
kuθra Yt. 22. 20 ; Yt. (Vtp.)
   24. 65.
kuda-δaēm Yt. 22. 8, 26 ; Yt.
   (Vtp.) 24. 55.
kudō-zātanąm[čiṯ N. 70.
kurō W. 2. 2 (2).
kəm N. 12.
kəm[čiṯ N. 105 ; T. 14.
kəmnā Phl. Vd. 11. 16, 18, 20 ;
   Vij. p. 67.
kərəta N. 33, 46. Cf. *ātarə°*
   and *tanu°*.
kərətaēibyō cf. *yasnō°*.
kərətanąm Vij. p. 127.
kərətahe Yt. (Vtp.) 24. 47.
kərətīš[ča N. 91.

kərətō cf. *zaranyō°*.
kərəθinō cf *aratō°*.
kərəθən N. 46.
kərəpəm[*ča* ZPGl. 11. 5.
kərənaoiti Ep. M. 1. 4. 3 ; Vij. p. 179.
kərənaoṯ Phl. Vd. 2. 19, 32.
kərənaomi Yt. (Vtp.) 24. 49.
kərənavantəm Yt. 22. 13 (2).
kərənavāṯ Yt. (APZ.) 23. 2.
kərənavāni Vij. p. 126.
kərənavāhi Yt. (Vtp.) 24. 3.
kərənuyāṯ Vij. p. 146.
kərəntaṯ cf. *frā°*.
kərənyō Yt. (Vtp.) 24. 37 (2).
kərənvantəm Yt. (Vtp.) 24. 59 (2).
kərəsāspəm Yt. (APZ.) 23. 3.
kərəsqm N. 26.
kərəsqs[*ča* N. 53.
kərəstō cf. *frā°*.
kərəšå N. 101.
kəhrpa N. 59 (2); Phl. Vd. 3. 40; T. 65; Yt. 22. 9 (2),

10; Yt. (Vtp.) 24. 1, 56 (2), 57. Cf. *tanu°*.
kəhrpayå N. 59.
kəhrpahe N. 106.
kəhrpəm Yt. (APZ.) 23. 3.
* kəhrpąm N. 47 (emended from [*aspō*] *karp ām*).
kə̄ N. 97. Cf. *hāθrākəbiš*.
kə̄s[*ča* N. 92.
kō N. 13, 41; Phl. Ys. 9. 27; Vij. p. 53; ZPGl. 17. 9.
kåṇhāmaide Yt. (Vtp.) 24. 22.
kąm Vij. p. 57.
kąm[*čiṯ* N. 97.
kąhya N. 54.
ktarā[*čiṯ* N. 23.
knmō N. 1.
kva HtN. p. 485 (2); SlS. 13. 6; Yt. 22. 1, 3, 5, 19, 39; Yt. (Vtp.) 24. 53.
kvaē N. 103.
kva[*čiṯ* N. 108.
kvaṯ N. 103.

x.

xayə̄uš Yt. (Vtp.) 24. 1.
xavō cf. *hapsnāi-apnō-°*.
xūxti T. 46 (read *hūxti*).
xə̄ṯ N. 44.
xraoiði Phl. Vd. 13. 34.
xrataoṯ T. 55.
xratum cf. *duš°*.
xratumå ZPGl. 19. 7.
xratuš ZPGl. 31. 7. Cf. *aδāityō*.
xratūm N. 11, 84; Yt. 22. 38; Yt. 24. 41.

xratūm[*ča* N. 52.
xratə̄uš Yt. (Vtp.) 24. 41.
xraθwa N. 40; T. 35. Cf. *kasu°* and *duš°*.
xrayāaṯ[*ča* N. 67.
xrasyō ZPGl. 39. 1.
xrāyō Dk. (P. Sj.) 3. 156.
xružda ZPGl. 8. 10.
xrə N. 91.
xrvantəm A: 28; Yt. 22. 17, 35; Yt. (Vtp.) 24. 63.

xrvī Pars. p. 534.

xšaudrəm N. 64.

xšaētahe cf. *x°arə°*.

xšaētō Yt. (APZ.) **23**. 3 ; ZPGl. 18. 11.

xšaēnō cf. *a°*.

xšaθra AG. 7 ; Yt. (Vtp.) **24**. 47. Cf. *aratu°, ratu°* and *hu°*.

xšaθraēibyō Phl. Vd. **4**. 10.

xšaθrata W. **8**. 2.

xšaθrahe Dk. (P. Sj.) 3. 156.

xšaθrā Dk. (P. Sj.) 3. 131.

xšaθrā[*ča* W. **1**. 1.

xšaθrāṭ T. 31; Yt. (Vtp.) **24**. 35.

xšaθrəm N. 34; W. **9**. 1 ; Yt. (Vtp.) **24**. 46, 48 (2).

xšaθrəm[*ča* N. 46 (3), 70.

xšaθrəm[*čā* Phl. Ys. **27** end ; T. 70; W. **9**. 2.

xšaθre T. 48.

xšaθrō N. 46, 47 ; ZPGl. 18. 10.

xšaθrō-činaṇhō Ep. M. **1**. 4. 3 (note).

xšaθrąm ZPGl. 11. 8.

xšadrəm N. 64 read *xšāu°*.

xšapa A. 51.

xšapaṭ N. 46, 50. (*Haug* in ZPGl. 78. 12 reads *xšapāṭ*.)

xšapanəm Yt. **22**. 1, 2, 3, 4, 5, 6, 19, 20; Yt. (Vtp.) **24**. 41 (2), 53, 54.

xšapanąm Phl. Vd. **7**. 52 (2).

xšaparəm N. 47.

xšape N. 51.

xšapō SlS. **13**. 43 ; Yt. **22**. 7, 25 ; Yt. (Vtp.) **24**. 55.

xšaprāṭ Vij. p. 179.

xšafa ZPGl. 42. 6.

xšafne Yt. **22**. 38.

xšafnō N. 4.

xšafnąm[*ča* N. 4.

xšayaṭ-vaxš ZPGl. **8**. 11.

xšayantəm Yt. (Vtp.) **24**. 23.

xšayamana Vij. p. 89 (2) ; ZPGl. 11. 9 ; 18. 11.

xšayamna Yt. (Vtp.) **24**. 35.

xšayāṭ W. **4**. 2.

xšayeta Yt. (Vtp.) **24**. 47.

xšayeti Yt. (Vtp.) **24**. 47.

xšayeni W. **4**. 2.

xšayō ZPGl. 18. 10.

xšayąs cf. *vasə°*.

xšavaidīm Vij. p. 127.

xšavaš T. 8 ; Vij. p. 126.

xšāudrinąm N. 67.

xšāudrəm N. 66.

xšāurunəm N. 64.

xšim ZPGl. 19. 3.

xšuiδa ZPGl. 18. 13.

xšudra[*ča* T. 94.

xšudrim N. 64.

xšudru N. 61.

xšudrā̊ N. 11 ; Vth. 3, 8 ; ZPGl. 11. 2.

xšuvisti Phl. Vd. **2**. 32 (v. l. *xšivisti*).

xšōiθnyā̊ Yt. **22**. 9 ; Yt. (Vtp.) **24**. 56.

xšōiθra Yt. (Vtp.) **24**. 35.

xštāṭ ZPGl. 19. 3.

xštum ZPGl. **1**. 8.

xštūm N. 82.

xštamičaṭ[ča Phl. Vd. 1. 14.

xštvi Vij. p. 138.

xštvō N. 102.

xšnaoθra N. 28 (2), 37, 46 (6), 47, 48, 58, 61 (2), 67, 103 ; Vij. p. 79, 128, 153, 159, 162, 164, 165 ; W. 2. 1 ; 6. 1 (3); 7. 1.

xšnaoθrāi[ča N. 58, 61, 81 ; Pars. p. 521.

xšnaoθrəm W. Yt. 21. 5.   Cf. also *spnāθrəm*.

xšnaōšta T. 107.

xšnāvayeiti Ep. M. 1. 4. 3 (2).

xšnāvayeite T. 107.

xšnuta ZPGl. 19. 1.

xšnūitīm[ča T. 89.

xšnūtō Yt (Vtp.) 24. 38.

xšnūtā̊ CB (3).

xšnūmaine N. 47 (5), 61 ; Vij. p. 128, 141.

xšvaēpaya Phl. Ys. 9. 35.

xšvaš AG. 6 ; N. 4, 50, 67, 103 ; ZPGl. 1. 8.   Cf. *xšavaš*.

xšvaš-mā̊nhā Dk. 8. 44. 27 ; Phl. Vd. 9. 32, 130[a].

xšviptavaiti Yt. (Vtp.) 24. 49.

xšviptyō[vā Yt. (Vtp.) 24. 13.

g.

gainti- cf. *duž°*.

gaintīs[ča Yt. 22. 25.

gairi-masō Phl. Vd. 5. 9.

gairīm N. 47 ; W. 5. 2 ; Yt. 22. 38.

gaēiθya W. 1. 2.

gaēθa cf. *frādaṭ°* and *hapō°*.

gaēθanąm AG. 9 ; N. 2 (2), 3 (2) ; W. Yt. 21. 1 ; Yt. 22. 1 ; ZPGl. 15. 11.   Cf. *haðō°*.

gaēθābyō N. 2 ; T. 15 ; Vij. p. 145.

gaēθāhvō A. 48.

gaēθā̊ N. 3, 5 (3), 31, 44 ; Phl. Vd. 8. 72 ; 9. 27 ; Yt. (Vtp.) 24. 15.

gaēθąm A. 81 ; Vij. p. 24.

gaēm N. 83 ; ZPGl. 31. 2; 41. 3.

gaēsa ZPGl. 6. 7.

gaodana N. 64 (4).

gaoðanəm Yt. (Vtp.) 24. 49.

gaona cf. *paouru°*.

gaonanąm A. 17.

gaonavatō N. 65.

gaonahe N. 65.

gaonəm ZPGl. 6. 6, 8.

gaom A. 82.

gaomaitibyas[ča Yt. 22. 16, 34.

gaomavaitanąm[ča Vij. p. 89.

gaomavaitibyas[ča Yt. (Vtp.) 24. 62.

gaomavaitibyō Vij. p. 127.

gaomavaitīm N. 46.

gaoyaotōiš Vij. p. 126.

gaosūrəm Yt. (Vtp.) 24. 9.

gaoš Yt. (Vtp.) 24. 45 ; ZPGl. 9. 11.

gaoša T. 59.

gaošaēibyō T. 59.

gaošəm N. 65.

gaošō N. 46.   Cf. *asruṯ°*.

gaošąm cf. *sraota°*.

gaōspånta T. 71.

gaōhudå T. 71.

gatə̄e ZPGl. 30. 10.

gatvō Yt. (Vtp.) **24**. 60.

gaθåbyō N. 31.

gaθąm N. 46.

gaðō A. 80.

gaðōitīš[ča N. 53.

gaðwa W. **2**. 2.

gantumō N. 28.

gaya ZPGl. 14. 12.

gayanti cf. *pairi°*.

gayehe W. Yt. **21**. 15.

gayehe-marata ZPGl. 15. 1.

gayehē Phl. Ys. **9**. 4.   Cf. *apa°*.

gayō W. **4**. 3.

garəðma cf. *aiwi°*.

garəmō-varanhəm AG. 7.

garəžda ZPGl. 31. 3.

garō Yt. (Vtp.) **24**. 28, 33, 39.

garōiš N. 47, 65.

garō-nmānəm SlS. **13**. 8.

gava N. 18, 76; ZPGl. 31. 1.   Cf. *darəγō°*.

gavanahe N. 101.

gavanąm N. 42 (v. l. *gavaąm*).

gavastryā N. 85.

gavā Phl. Vd. **1**. 4.

gavāstra[ča N. 52.

gavāstryā[ča N. 60.

gavāstryāvarəza ZPGl. 31. 4.

[*gave*] Phl. Vd. **19**. 41.

gave Yt. (Vtp.) **24**. 41.

gavō A. 84; Māh. Yt. 5.

gavąm ZPGl. 12. 2.

gāim ZPGl. 41. 3.   •

gāuš N. 17. 28; Phl. Vd. **2**. 10; T. 92, 93; Vij. p. 126.

gātaoṯ T. 39.

gātava N. 81 (3).

gātubyō VS. Extr. 1, 2, 3, 4.

gātum ZPGl. 14. 6.

gātum[ča ZPGl. 13. 11.

gātuš N. 79, 103.   Cf. *dāityō°*.

gātūm N. 81 (2).

gātō Pars. p. 522.

gātvō A. 12; Yt. **22**. 14 (2).

gāθanąm N. 22 (4), 25, 26, 30 (2), 37, 38, 39, 42, 43, 44, 46, 47, 49, 50, 51, 103.

gāθanąm[čiṯ N. 22.

gāθayå N. 102; Yt. (Vtp.) **24**. 53.

gāθā N. 96.

gāθābiš N. 4.

gāθābyō N. 31 (2), 61; Vij. p. 55, 57, 72 (2), 186.

gāθāhva N. 33.

gāθå N. 22, 23, 26, 27, 32, 33, 41, 42 (2), 43, 44, 45, 85, 103.   Cf. *srutō°*.

gāθås[ča N. 48; Vij. p. 166; W. **7**. 2; Yt. **22**. 13; Yt. (Vtp.) **24**. 59.

gāθąm A. 81; Vij. p. 139; Yt. **22**. 2; Yt. (Vtp.) **24**. 54.

gāθwōiš T. 111.

gāθwō-štačaṯ ZPGl. 31. 3.

gāθwya Yt. (Vtp.) **24**. 39.

gāθwyąm Yt. 22. 20.

gām- cf. *aiwi°* and *θri°*.

gāma N. 103 ; Yt. 22. 15 (4),
27–33 ; Yt. (Vtp.) 24. 61
(3).

gāmanąm T. 39.

gāmahya ZPGl. 43. 5.

gāməm ZPGl. 43. 5.

gāman ZPGl. 41. 6.

gārōiš W. 5. 1.

gāvayanąm [*ča* N. 67.

gāvayayaiš N. 67.

gāvō cf. *pouru°*.

guðra ZPGl. 31. 1.

guðrā-sanhō ZPGl. 8. 9.

gušta ZPGl. 9. 9 ; 31. 2.

gūštā T. 4.

gərə Phl. Vd. 5. 19 (cf. *yāgərə?*).

gərəoa ZPGl. 31. 2.

gərəptahe VS. Extr. 3.

gərəptāi VS. Extr. 1.

gərəptəm VS. Extr. 2. Cf. *uz°*.

gərəf- cf. *api°* and *han°*.

gərəftayāt̰ N. 17.

gərəftəm N. 67.

gərəbyāt̰ N. 67.

gərəwnat̰ ZPGl. 30. 10.

gərəwyaite Yt. (Vtp.) 24. 30.

gərəwyeiti Yt. (Vtp.) 24. 30.

gərəmbayąn N. 71. Cf. *uz°*.

gərəmyāi cf. *pairi°*

gərəsnāvayō cf. *uz°*.

gərəzānå CB.

gə̄ ZPGl. 31. 1.

gə̄urvayāt̰ cf. *uz°*.

gə̄urvayeiti Phl. Vd. 4. 1.

gə̄uš N. 18, 47, 52, 53, 58, 60
(2), 65, 67 (4), 71, 108 ; Vij.
p. 83, 125, 155 ; W. 6. 1
(9) ; W. Yt. 21. 5 ; Yt.
(Vtp.) 24. 6, 31, 38.

gə̄uš [*ča* N. 60 (2).

gō cf. *pouru-gō*.

gå-stavå A. 78.

gås [*ča* N. 72 (read *gāθås* [*ča*).

gąm N. 102 ; W. Yt. 21. 3 ;
ZPGl. 31. 3.

gąm [*ča* Vij. p. 126, 137.

grəhmō ZPGl. 30. 10.

γ.

γanahe Yt. (Vtp.) 24. 50.

γanānå Yt. (Vtp.) 24. 29.

γənå Vij. p. 99 ; ZPGl. 31. 5.

γnat̰ ZPGl. 31. 5.

γnāt̰ ZPGl. 31. 5.

γnixta cf. *aiwi°*

γnyāi Vth. 10.

γmatəm cf. *ni°*.

č.

ča A. 1 (3) ; AG. 10 ; BkN. p.
471 (2) ; CB (3) ; FD. 7 (2) ;
N. 3 (5), 4 (3), 6 (2), 8 (4), 9
(2), 11 (3), 12, 22, 24 (2),
29, 33 (2), 34, 37, 40 (3),
45 (2), 46 (17), 47 (11), 48
(11), 49 (2), 50 (3), 52 (3),
53 (5), 56, 57 (4), 58 (2), 59

(2), 60 (6), 61 (3), 63, 65 (4), 67 (5), 68 (3), 70 (3), 71 (2), 72 (4), 73 (3), 74 (3), 75 (3), 76 (2), 81 (8), 82, 83 (2), 84 (8), 87, 91 (3), 92 (3), 94, 95 (6), 97 (5), 98 (2), 99 (2), 103 (2), 109; Pars. p. 521 (5), 531 (5), 532 (5), 534 (3), 535; Pl. 1 (3), 2, 5, 7, 10; Phl. Vd. 1. 14 (4), 20; 5, 9; 7. 52 (5); Phl. Ys. 31. 20; 51 end; SlS. 13. 1; T. 23, 28 (2), 35 (2), 36 (6), 37, 39, 45, 47 (2), 57 (3), 58 (3), 60 (2), 61, 64, 71 (2), 75, 76, 77 (2), 83 (3), 84, 88 (7), 89 (5), 90, 93, 94 (5), 100 (2), 108, 123; Vij. p. 23, 24, (3), 83 (2), 89 (7), 96, 97, 99, 112 (2), 126, 127, 128 (4), 134, 137, 148 (2), 156 (2), 158 (2), 164 (2), 165 (2), 166 (3), 179 (3), 181; W. 1. 1–2 (8); 2. 1–3 (3), 3; 5. 1–2 (6); 7. 1–2 (8); 8. 1 (2); W. Yt. 21 1 (3), 6 (3), 7 (6), 8 (3), 10 (3), 11 (6), 12 (3), 13 (6), 14 (3), 16 (8), 17 (3); Yt. 22. 6, 7, 10, 11 (6), 12, 13 (10), 14 (2), 16 (3), 17 (2), 25 (2), 34 (4), 35 (2), 36, 40; Yt. (APZ.) 23. 8; Yt. (Vtp.) 24. 6, 8 (2), 10 (4), 14 (3) 15 (4), 18 (2), 23, 27 (2), 28 (3), 29 (2), 30 (5), 32 (2), 33, 34 (6), 35, 36 (2), 37 (6),

38, 40 (4), 41 (2), 42, 43 (3), 46 (5), 47 (4), 49 (2), 51, 52 (2), 57, 58 (7), 59 (9), 60 (2), 62 (4), 63 (2); ZPGl. 6. 3, 4 (2); 10. 11; 11. 5, 6, 10 (2); 13. 5, 6, 11, 12; 15. 12; 16. 8; 17. 4, 5 (3), 6 (2); 21. 7; 29. 1; 39. 4; 40. 7; 41. 6.

ča(θwārō?) N. 60.

čaiti N. 65; Phl. Vd. 5. 19; ZPGl. 29. 7.

čaētənti ZPGl. 29. 6.

čakana Yt. 22. 11, 12; Yt. (Vtp.) 24. 58; ZPGl. 29. 7.

čaxrvaiθyā̊ A. 81.

čataɳrō N. 65, 102.

čati[*ča* T. 64.

čaturąm N. 65.

čaθrāyāim FD. 5; SlS. 13. 17.

čaθruš SlS. 13. 43.

čaθrušāmrūta[*ča* N. 33, 36.

čaθrušəm N. 42.

čaθwarə Vij. p. 137; ZPGl. 15. 10.

čaθwarəsatəm N. 65.

čaθwārəstəm[*ča* Vij. p. 179.

čaθwārō N. 66, 69; Vij. p. 136 (°*warō*), 179 (2).

*čaθwārō N. 60 (emendation of *ča θwārō*.).

čat[*ča* ZPGl. 40. 7.

čantifratufriš N. 100.

čanvatō T. 2. (read *činvatō*).

čayąn N. 1.

čar- cf. *para*°, *fra*° and *vī*°.

čaranaya cf. *sraošõ°*.

čarāitinąm Yt. **22.** 10; Yt. (Vtp.) **24.** 57.

čarāitiš Yt. **22.** 10; Yt. (Vtp.) **24.** 57.

čarətutārō ZPGl. 29. 7.

čarətu-drājō ZPGl. 29. 5.

čarəte N. 66.

čarətąm ZPGl. 29. 5.

čarəθrå cf. *frašõ°*.

čarədayå cf. *paouru°*.

[*čarənta*] v. l. N. 52.

čarəmanąm [*ča* N. 58.

čarəmąn [*ča* N. 95.

čavaiti ZPGl. 41. 5.

čašāiti N. 17.

čašte N. 17.

čašmanå T. 71.

čahmāi N. 11.

čahmi FD. 3 (2).

čā N. 22, 28 (2), 65 ; Pars. p. 541 (*čå*); Phl. Vd. **3.** 14 ; **9.** 12 (2); Phl. Ys. **27** end; SlS. **13.** 1 ; T. 4 (2), 6 (2), 30 (2) 31 (3), 38, 70 (2), 115 (2); Vij. p. 156, 159; W. **8.** 1, 2 ; **9.** 3 (2) ZPGl. 13. 6; 14. 8.

čārąm ZPGl. 29. 7.

čiąkaδavatọ ZPGl. 10. 3.

čikaēn ZPGl. 3. 5, 7, 8.

čikayatō ZPGl. 3. 5, 7 ; 7. 8.

čikayaṯ Yt. (Vtp.) **24.** 44 ; ZPGl. 3. 3.

[*čikčθrəm*] v. l. N. 67.

čiči ZPGl 14. 4.

čiθa ZPGl. 29. 6.

čiθaya Yt. (Vtp.) **24.** 44 (2).

čiθayaē [*ča* N. 45.

čiθiāi T. 18.

čiθīm N. 52.

čiθwarō Vij. p. 148.

čiθra Yt. (Vtp.) **24.** 7 ; ZPGl. 29. 6. Cf. *aša°*, *ašõ°* and *raēvas°*.

čiθra-vaṁhąm Yt. (Vtp.) **24.** 6 (2).

čiθrəm CB. (2); N. 67 ; W. **3.** 2 ; Yt. **22.** 40 ; Yt. (Vtp.) **24.** 8, 9.

čiθrəm [*ča* N. 65.

čiθre T. 108.

čiθrō Phl. Vd. 1. 14 (2).

čiθrå T. 75.

čiṯ A. 17, 41; N. 41, 46 (2), 51, 65, 67, 70, 83 ; Phl. Vd. 1. 14 ; **2.** 5 ; **7.** 52 ; SkN. p. 480 ; T. 11 (2), 14, 25, 40 (2), 48 (2), 65, 87, 98, 111, 114, 116, 122 ; Vij. p. 148 ; W, Yt. **21.** 5 ; Yt. **22.** 2, 4, 6 ; Yt. (Vtp.) **24.** 8, 9, 23, 30, 41, 47, 55 ; ZPGl. 2. 9 ; 8. 8 ; 12. 7 ; 13. 5 ; 18. 8 ; 38. 10 ; 40. 7.

čina T. 39. Cf. *aēvā°* and *ya-zōiš°*.

činaiemi ZPGl. 29. 8. (R. reads *bin°*.)

činaṇhō. Cf. *xšaθrō°*.

činəm N. 14.

činma T. 98 (2).

činmanō ZPGl. 29. 8.

činvatō Yt. (Vtp.) **24**. 42.
činvaṯ Vij. p. 25.
činvaṯ-pərətūm Vth. 14.
čim A. 48 (4).
čiryō A. 84.
čistiš ZPGl. 29. 8.
čiš A. 58 ; N. 72, 100 (2) (read *haθra*°), 101 ; Phl. Vd. **5**. 34 ; T. 4, 18, 68 ; W. **4**. 2 ; **8**. 1.
čišānāi[*ča* N. 84.
čiš[*ča* Yt. **22**. 10, 11 ; Yt. (Vtp.) **24**. 57, 58.
čište T. 3.
čištōiš N. 47.

čīčarəná̌ Yt. (Vtp.) **24**. 54.
čūčiš cf. *afra*.
čīṯ N. 60.
čīm cf. *mā*°.
čōiṯ N. 84.
čōišta T. 48.
čá̌ (for *čā*) Pars. p. 541.
čyāɣantō N. 108.
čyá̌ N. 90.
čvaiti N. 17, 20.
čvaṯ N. 4 (2), 8, 9, 11, 27, 31, 65, 66, 67, 85, 89, 106, 109 ; Phl. Vd. **18**. 43 ; Vij. p. 23.
čvaṯbya N. 108.
čvantəm Phl. Vd. **2**. 19.

ĵ.

jaitīm cf. *paiti*°.
jaite Yt. (APZ.) **23**. 1 (3).
jaiδyata Yt. (Vtp.) **24**. 8.
jaiδyaṯ ZPGl. 27. 8.
jainti N. 45.
jau ZPGl. 37. 8.
jaē ZPGl. 4. 10.
jaēš ZPGl. 27. 9.
jaxšavá̌ ZPGl. 27. 7.
jaɣaurvatąm N. 67.
jaɣāra N. 19.
jaɣārayantəm Yt. (Vtp.) **24**. 41
jataṅhaṯ ZPGl. 27. 8.
jaθanō Vij. p. 151.
jafra ZPGl. 27. 7.
jaṅhōiṯ cf. *paiti*°.
janaiti Phl. Vd. **18**. 2.
janaṯ Phl. Vd. **7**. 52 (2).
janō cf. *aēvō*°.

janá̌ṅha N. 17.
jamanəm cf. *han*°.
jamyāṯ A. 111 ; AG. 10 ; N. 20, 28 (2), 46 ; Yt. (Vtp.) **24**. 34.
jayaṯ T. 118.
jayantəm cf. *dušmainyū*°.
jaraδiš T. 60.
jarəta ZPGl. 27. 9.
javaiti ZPGl. 14. 12.
javā Phl. Ys. **64**. 48 (Sp.)
jas- cf. *aipi*°, *apa*°, *us*°, *paiti*°, *pairi*°, *ni*°, *vī*°, and *han*°.
jasaṯ Yt. (Vtp.) **24**. 39.
jasāi Yt. (Vtp.) **24**. 22.
jasāṯ N. 82 ; T. 45 (2), 47.
jasən Phl. Vd. **1**. 14.
jasəntəm T. 10 (D. reads °*sánt*°); Yt. **22**. 13 ; Yt. (Vtp.) **24**. 59.

jasəntəm Vij. p. 89.

jasō N. 47.

jasōiθyā̊ W. Yt. 21. 5.

jasōiṯ Vij. p. 89.

jažuš FD. 3 ; Phl. Vd. 5. 32.

·*jahikāyāi* Yt. 22. 36.

jahikayā̊ T. 9.

jahī ZPGl. 5. 1.

[*jahmi*] v. l. FD. 3.

jāmāspaēibya Yt. (Vtp.) 24. 11.

jāmāspānahe FD. 7.

jāmāspō N. 89 ; Yt. (APZ.) 23.
 2 (2) ; Yt. (Vtp.) 24. 3.

jāmyāṯ Yt. (APZ.) 23. 8.

jigaurva Yt. 22. 8, 26.

jināiti ZPGl. 27.6.

jinō cf. *varo°*.

jimaiti ZPGl. 14. 10.

jimama Yt. (Vtp.) 24. 32.

jimāṯ ZPGl. 27. 7.

jirō cf. *pouru°*.

jivaiti Yt. (Vtp.) 24. 1 (2).

jivayəm Vij. p. 137.

jītayō N. 69 ; Phl. Ys. 38. 15
 (Sp.). Cf. *mərəzu°*.

jīti cf. *us°*, *darəγəm°*, *mərəzu°*,
 and *vohū°*.

jum ZPGl. 27. 6.

juye A. 53.

juyō Yt. 22. 2, 20.

jə̄ ZPGl. 4. 10.

jōis[*ča* Yt. (Vtp.) 24. 30.

jən cf. *vasō-jən-nāirīm*.

jvā̊ṅhō cf. *mərəzu°*.

t.

taurva N. 67.

[*taē*[*ča*] v. l. Phl. Vd. 5. 19.

taē[*ča* T. 108 ; Yt. (Vtp.) 24.
 15.

taē[*čiṯ* Phl. Vd. 1. 14.

taēčō Phl. Vd. 5. 49.

taēž- cf. *barōiθrō°*.

taošyeiti N. 100.

taožyā[*ča* Phl. Vd. 1. 19.

taxmanəm T. 45.

taxmahe N. 61.

taxməm Yt. (Vtp.) 24. 26.

taxmō A. 84 ; Yt. (APZ.) 23.
 2 ; Yt. (Vtp.) 24. 24, 25.

tač- cf. *anu°*, *usyəst°* and *han°*.

tača N. 37 ; ZPGl. 29. 1.

tačaintəm Vij. p. 89.

tačarəm ZPGl. 41. 11.

tačintiš A. 77.

taδa N. 54, 65, 69.

taδaō ZPGl. 41. 10.

taṯ A. 51 ; N. 12 (2), 30, 44,
 45, 48 (2), 51 (2), 54, 65, 68,
 103 (2) ; Phl. Vd. 2. 5 ; 7.
 52 ; 19. 10 ; T. 98 ; Vij. p.
 67 ; W. 9. 1 ; Yt. 22. 18 (2),
 36 (2) ; Yt. (Vtp.) 24. 38, 39,
 43, 46, 64 (3) ; ZPGl. 43. 5,
 6, 7, 8.

tapayeite cf. *ātāp°*.

tafnuš Yt. (Vtp.) 24. 50.

tanrō-piθwā̊ N. 15.

tanu N. 95.

tanu-kərəta Yt. (APZ.) 23. 1.

38 　　　　　　*tanu-kəhrpa — tištryehe*

tanu-kəhrpa Yt. (Vtp.) **24**. 1,
3.
tanupərəθa N. 38, 39 (2).
[*tanu*]-*pərəθanąm* N. 59.
tanu-pərəθahe N. 54.
tanupərəθāi N. 17, 18.
tanu-pərəθāṯ N. 16.
tanupərəθəm N. 39 (2), 105.
tanupərəθəhe T. 9.
tanupərəθō N. 38 (2), 39.
tanunąm T. 18 ; W. Yt. **21**. 5.
　Cf. *pərətō°*.
tanum ZPGl. 37. 5.
tanumazō T. 24 (2), 25.
tanu-mą̇θrahe N. 61.
tanumą̇θrō ZPGl. 29. 3.
tanuš A. 53 ; ZPGl. 24. 8 ; 37.
4.　Cf. *pəšō°*.
tanušu W. **4**. 3.
tanūm N. 7 (2), 41, 42 (2), 43 ;
　Vij. p. 89, 138, 148, 179 (2),
　180 ; Yt. (Vtp.) 24. 26, 40,
41.
tančištəm ZPGl. 29. 1.
tančištō T. 45.
tanva A. 48. Cf. *pəšō°*.
tanvaē[*ča* ZPGl. 11. 9.
tanvō A. 25, 26, 27, 28 ; T. 97 ;
　Vij. p. 112 ; Yt. **22**. 11 ; Yt.
　(Vtp.) **24**. 58. Cf. *srao°*.
tarainaəma.　Cf. *ātarə°*.
taraδāta ZPGl. 29. 4.
taraδātō N. 47.
taras[*ča* N. 95 ; Yt. (Vtp.) **24**.
　35, 36, 41 (2); ZPGl. 6. 4.
tarəwani W. **2**. 2.

tarəmanō ZPGl. 29. 2.
tarəmanō ZPGl. 29. 2.
tarō N. 42 (3), 65, 90, 100 (2),
　101; Vth. 14 ; Yt. (Vtp.) **24**.
　42.
tarō-piθwəm Yt. (Vtp.) **24**. 9.
tarōmaiti N. 41.
taršu[*ča* AG. 10 ; T. 94.
taršna N. 15 (2).
tava Dd. **43**. 2. 5 ; N. 37, 46
　(4), 48, 67, 70 (2); Vij. p.
　134, 141, 165 ; W. **6**. 1; 7.
　1; Yt. (APZ.) **23**. 1.
tavaṯ cf. *frā°*.
tanā[*čā* ZPGl. 14. 8.
tas[*čiṯ* T. 111.
tašaṯ ZPGl. 29. 4.
tašni N. 47.
tašne N. 67 ; W. **6**. 1 (3).
tahmō T. 104, 118.　Cf. *aš°*.
tā N. 40, 50.
tāitya cf. *ṣ̌yaoθanə°*.
tā[*ča* ZPGl. 29. 1.
tā[*čiṯ* N. 108.
tā[*čiṯ* N. 87.
tātō N. 61 ; ZPGl. 29. 1.
tāṯ N. 12.
tāya N. 15 ; ZPGl. 29. 3.
tāyuš N. 6, 63 (2).
tāyušå̄s[*ča* ZPGl. 39. 4.
tāyō ZPGl. 39. 4.
tāyå̄s[*ča* T. 36.
tāšta N. 66.
tinąm N. 95 (read *tanum* ?).
tištryehe N. 47 (6); Pars. p.
　535.

tišrō N. 42, 73, 100 (3), 101 (3); ZPGl. 1. 5.

tišrąm Phl. Vd. **7**. 52 (2).

tižinavantəm Yt. (APZ.) **23**. 6.

tižvantəm Yt. (Vtp.) **24**. 4.

tuθraēšu N. 68.

tum Yt. **22**. 12, 13 (2).

tū N. 34, 46; W. **8**. 1.

tūirinąm N. 66, 67.

tūirīm N. 11, 82; Yt. **22**. 15, 27–33; ZPGl. 1. 7.

tūirya Vij. p. 139.

tūiryanąm Phl. Vd. **3**. 42; **5**. 38; Vij. p. 148.

tūiryā N. 102 (2).

tūiryābiš Phl. Vd. **7**. 52.

tūiryehe T. 8.

tūiryō Vij. p. 138.

tūn Phl. Vd. **1**. 14.

tū-nō Yt. (Vtp.) **24**. 23.

tūm Yt. (Vtp.) **24**. 12, 13 (2), 22, 25, 31, 34, 36, 43, 57, 59; ZPGl. 29. 3. (R. reads *tum*.)

tūm[čiṯ Yt. (Vtp.) **24**. 9.

tūšiš ZPGl. 29. 3.

təm N. 42; W. **4**. 1; Yt. **22**. 8, 26; Yt. (Vtp.) **24**. 8, 42.

-təm N. 71 (in *frāyu . . . təm*).

təmaṇhahe A. 28.

təmahe N. 68.

təmōhva N. 19, 30; Yt. **22**. 27–33.

tərəsənti cf. *fra°*.

təvišīm N. 46.

tə̄ N. 48 (2); Vij. p. 165, 166.

tē N. 46 (3), 47 (2), 65; Phl. Vd. **17**. 9, 11; T. 54, 66, 69, 71, 90; Vij. p. 99, 133; W. **1**. 2; **4**. 1; **7**. 2; W. Yt. **21**. 1; Yt. **22**. 11, 12, 16, 34; Yt. (APZ.) **23**. 1 (3), 2, 5; Yt. (Vtp.) **24**. 3, 13, 18 (2), 19, 20, 32 (2), 34, 35, 36, 38, 41, 51, 52 (2), 58 (2), 62; ZPGl. **15**. 8; **16**. 10. Cf. *frā-tē*.

tə̊ N. 61, 103; T. 76; Yt. (Vtp.) **24**. 46.

tə̊ṇhrō T. 120.

tə̊s[čā W. **9**. 3.

tąm N. 10; Vij. p. 51; Yt. **22**. 13.

tčō N. 88.

tnaūm Vij. p. 67 (read *tanūm*).

tnāiš N. 58.

θ

θawərəštāra Vij. p. 54.

θanavanta ZPGl. 31. 7.

θanvas[ča N. 97.

θ[a]mananuhatąm Vij. p. 53.

θamanəm ZPGl. 31. 8.

θātuš Yt. (Vtp.) **24**. 18.

θwaxšitə̊ ZPGl. 15. 5.

θwaṯ Yt. (Vtp.) **24**. 51.

θwayaṇhəm N. 10 (3).

θwayeiti Yt. (Vtp.) **24**. 27.

θwarəsa cf. *ava°*.

θwarəšta T. 71.

θwarəsə̊s[ča N. 40.

θwarsō Phl. Vd. **2**. 19.

θwā N. 34, 47, 48; Phl. Vd. **19**. 10; Vij. p. 165; W. **7**. 2; Yt. (Vtp.) **24**. 13, 15, 20 (2), 21, 22, 26, 35, 37, 38, 45.
θwāiš N. 80.
θwāṯ N. 7.
θwārō N. 60 (read *čaθ°*).
θwāšahe N. 47; Yt. (Vtp.) **24**. 24.
θwirəsaiti N. 53.
θwərəs- cf. *a°*, *upa°* and *θaw°*.
θwərəšāiti N. 52.
θwəreštō Vij. p. 54.
θwōi N. 34.
θwąm CB; FD. 7; N. 105; Phl. Ys. **9**. 27; T. 30; Yt. **22**. 11; Yt. (Vtp.) **24**. 13, 35, 36, 38, 39, 41 (2), 43, 49, 58; ZPGl. 3. 10; 31. 7; 41. 6.
θnasaṯ Phl. Vd. **7**. 52.
θnātō ZPGl. 31. 6.
θraētaonahe W. **2**. 1, 3; ZPGl. 15. 8.
θraētaonəm W. **2**. 2.
θraētaonō Yt. (APZ.) **23**. 2.
θraošta Yt. **22**. 7, 25; Yt. (Vtp.) **24**. 55.
θraxti N. 70.
θraxtim N. 74.
θraxtiš N. 73.
θraxtəm N. 79.
θraŋ ZPGl. 31. 8.
θraŋhibyō T. 59.
θrayana[ča T. 94.
θrayąm N. 108; T. 39; ZPGl. 1. 6.
θraviṯ T. 38.
θrātōtəmō Yt. (Vtp.) **24**. 18.
θrāθrahs T. 100 (read *θrāθraŋhas[ča*).
θrāθrā ZPGl. 31.6.
θrāyō T. 99; Vij. p. 138, 157; Yt. (APZ.) **23**. 5 (3); Yt. (Vtp.) **24**. 3 (3).
θrāyōsata ZPGl. 31. 9.
θri N. 42, 43, 69 (2), 109 (3).
θrixšaparəm N. 2, 4.
θrixšafarəm N. 11.
θrigāmahe N. 69.
θrigāmi N. 83 (2).
θrigāməm ZPGl. 43. 5.
θritīm N. 82; Yt. **22**. 15; Yt. (Vtp.) **24**. 61; ZPGl. 1. 5.
θrityā N. 102.
θrityehe T. 8.
θrityō N. 2; Vij. p. 138; Yt. (Vtp.) **24**. 23.
θrityå N. 11, 42; Yt. **22**. 7, 23; Yt. (Vtp.) **24**. 55.
θrityąm Yt. **22**. 5, 21; Yt. (Vtp.) **24**. 54.
θripiθwō SkN. p. 480.
θripiθwōδi ZPGl. 38. 5 (R. reads *°wozi*).
θrimō Yt. (Vtp.) **24**. 49.
θriyaxštiš[ča ZPGl. 16. 8.
θri-vačahim ZPGl. 43. 4.
θrisa N. 108.
θrisatəm AG. 8.
θrisąs[ča Yt. (Vtp.) **24**. 18.

θristəm ZPGl. 31. 9.

θriš N. 4, 31 (2), 41, 66, 67, 88, 90, 97 (3).

θrišāmrūta N. 33.

θrišūm N. 4, 42, 43.

θriš[čiṯ T. 87; Yt. (Vtp.) 24. 41.

θrizantūm Phl. Vd. 1. 16.

θrizarəmaēm N. 11.

θrī N. 83; T. 7, 8.

θrīšva ZPGl. 1. 6.

θrəuitasti N. 85.

θrəməm[ča Pars. p. 531 (read θri°).

θrəsarəm T. 60.

θrəsarəm[ča T. 60.

θrəstəməm cf. apa° and upa°·

θrəfðō ZPGl. 31. 6.

θryas[ča Yt. (Vtp.) 24. 18.

θryąm N. 65, 105 (2).

d.

daiti Phl. Vd. 13. 34.

daiθyāṯ Yt.(Vtp.) 24. 9.

daiðīṯ N. 18 (v. l. daiðiṯ).

daiðiš Yt. (Vtp.) 24. 48 (2).

daiðyama Yt. (Vtp.) 24. 58.

daēum Yt. (Vtp.) 24. 26.

daēna N. 71; Yt. 22. 9, 11 (2); Yt. (Vtp.) 24. 35, 52, 56, 58. Cf. aγa°, duž° and hu°.

daēna[ča W. Yt. 21. 4.

daēnayāṯ N. 41 (2).

daēnayå SlS. 13. 1; T. 20; Yt. (Vtp.) 24. 42.

daēnayås[ča Yt. (Vtp.) 24. 10, 34, 37.

daēne N. 3 (3).

daēnå N. 70.

daēnąm HtN. p. 484; Phl. Vd. 5. 19; Vij. p. 126.

daēnąm[ča Yt. (Vtp.) 24. 10, 14.

daēnyå Vth. 2, 7.

daēm cf. kuda°.

daēva A. 19; N. 68; Phl. Vd. 2. 5; W. 4. 3.

daēvanąm N. 33; Pars. p. 535 (2).

daēvayaṯ ZPGl. 27. 1.

daēvayasnaēibyō N. 54.

daēvayasnanąm HtN. p. 484; N. 59.

daēvayasnanąm[ča N. 11.

daēvayasnahe N. 11.

daēvayasnāi N. 17, 18.

daēvayasnāṯ N. 16.

daēvayasnəm N. 105; Phl. Vd. 7. 52.

daēvayasne Phl. Vd. 7. 43.

daēvayasnō T. 9.

daēvayasnąm Yt. (Vtp.) 24. 26.

daēvīm A. 28.

daēvīš[ča N. 53.

daēsayama Yt. (Vtp.) 24. 32.

daēsayāṯ Yt. (Vtp.) 24. 42.

daēsayeni T. 82.

daomna Yt. 22. 42.

daoša ZPGl. 10. 2.

daošatarəm Phl. Vd. 1. 18.

daožaṅhahe A. 28.

daožaṇhum T. 93.
daōnō-jaitiš N. 67 (v. l. *naonō°* read *baoδō°*).
daxma Vij. p. 139, 179 (2).
daⱡmanąm Vij. p. 146.
daxmō ZPGl. 27. 1.
daxša T. 37.
daxšamaēštam N. 70.
daxšta ZPGl. 27. 2.
daxštō Phl. Vd. 1. 13.
daxšmaitiš ZPGl. 41. 8.
dataras[*čiṯ* Yṭ. (Vtp.) 24. 47.
datəm cf. *ahuraδ°*.
datå N. 101.
daθaite Yt. (Vtp.) 24. 50.
daθaṯ T. 64; Yt. (Vtp.) 24. 25.
daθāi cf. *fra°*.
daθāiti T. 74; ZPGl. 13. 9.
daθānō N. 37; T. 10.
daθuš AG. 9.
daθušō CB.; N. 46, 47 (3); Yt. (Vtp.) 24. 46, 51.
dadəmaide T. 30.
daδaiti Vth. 16, 17.
daδaoiš Yt. (Vtp.) 24. 50.
daθaṯ W. 9. 2.
daδaṇha ZPGl. 11. 2.
daδāiti N. 17, 25 (2), 37, 61, 62, 84, 101, 105 (2); Vth. 5 (2); Yt. (Vtp.) 24. 34, 46, 48; ZPGl. 13. 9.
daδāite T. 110.
daδāṯ Yt. (Vtp.) 24. 31.
daδō T. 110.
daδąmi N. 20, 28, 46; Vij. p. 74.

daδvå Vij. p. 50, 51 (3), 52, 54.
dadvåṇhəm Vij. p. 52 (2).
daṭaiti T. 44.
dapas[*ča* N. 68.
danuhu cf. *uz°*.
daṇrō ZPGl. 9. 6.
daṇhaoṯ N. 8.
[*daṇhāvō*] Phl. Vd. 19. 41.
daṇhupatayō A. 59.
daṇhu-baxtəm T. 95.
daṇhuš Phl. Vd. 2. 10.
daṇhōuš[*ča* N. 8.
daṇhōṯ N. 8 (v. l. *daṇhōiṯ*).
daṇhåsčāuiṯ N. 102.
daṇhrəm Vij. p. 24.
daṇhrō ZPGl. 8. 7.
daṇhvō N. 8; T. 22.
daṅhāurvaēsahe Yt. (Vtp.) 24. 17.
daṅhištaēšva Yt. (Vtp.) 24. 42.
daṅhu-paiti Yt. (APZ.) 23. 1.
daṅhu-paitiš Yt. (Vtp.) 24. 48.
daṅhupatōiš Yt. (Vtp.) 24. 16.
daṅhēuš Phl. Vd. 1. 19; Yt. (APZ.) 23. 2; Yt. (Vtp.) 24. 16, 48.
daṅhve ZPGl. 12.2.
dantānō ZPGl. 8. 3.
daya HtN. p. 485; SlS. 13. 6; Vij. p. 134.
dayō cf. *paiti°*.
daraite cf. *han°*.
daraonō Vij. p. 89, 99, 136 (2).
daraoš Pars. p. 534.
daran- cf. *uši°*.

darājạn W. 8. 1.
darᵊγa T. 120.
darᵊγāi Yt. (Vtp.) 24. 32 (2).
darᵊγᵊm Yt. 22. 16, 34; Yt. (Vtp.) 24. 62; ZPGl. 11. 10, 12.
darᵊγᵊm-jīti Yt. (APZ.) 23. 1; Yt. (Vtp.) 24. 1.
darᵊγō-gava Yt. 22. 42.
darᵊγō-yaštīm [*ča* Yt. (Vtp.) 24. 60.
darᵊγō-yaštᵊm [*ča* Yt. 22. 14.
darᵊtō N. 15.
darᵊθrāi Yt. 22. 38.
darᵊθrᵊm T. 51.
dᵊrᵊvaṯ ZPGl. 27. 2.
darᵊsa T. 123.
darᵊši-draoš N. 61.
darᵊzayaēiti N. 99 (v. l. °*yeiti*).
darᵊzᵊra ZPGl. 27. 3.
darš cf. *parō°*.
dava T. 116.
[*davaisne*] v. l. Phl. 7. 42. (Read *daēvayasne*.)
davata FD. 7; Yt. (Vtp.) 24. 43.
davōsa Yt. (Vtp.) 24. 44.
dasa Vij. p. 179 (2); W. Yt. 21. 6; Yt. (APZ.) 23. 5; Yt. (Vtp.) 24. 3. Cf. *panča°*.
dasā N. 42.
dasta Yt. (Vtp.) 24. 6 (3), 8.
dasti N. 84, 105 (3).
dasmahe ZPGl. 1. 9.
dasvarᵊ Yt. (Vtp.) 24. 39.
dasvarᵊm W. 9. 2.

dasvā N. 46.
dašanᵊm N. 79.
dašina N. 65.
dašināṯ N. 79.
dašinᵊm N. 79.
dašinō ZPGl. 9. 11.
dašᵊnᵊm N. 65.
daš [*ča* ZPGl. 41. 6.
dazdā T. 114.
dazdi ZPGl. 27. 2.
dazde N. 55.
dazdyāi Pars. p. 534.
dažaṯ ZPGl. 27. 3.
dahākāi v. l. Phl. Vd. 1. 15; Yt. (APZ.) 23. 3.
dahma N. 39; T. 65.
dahmanąm N. 40, 105 (2).
dahmayāṯ SlS. 13. 43.
dahmayằ N. 61.
dahmahe N. 11, 104.
dahmāi N. 19.
dahmi Yt. (Vtp.) 24. 1.
dahmᵊm N. 12, 44, 45; Yt. (Vtp.) 24, 44.
dahmō N. 17, 19, 25, 27, 30, 37, 38, 39 (2), 104 (2); T. 64; Yt. (APZ.) 23. 1; ZPGl. 27. 1.
dahmąm T. 66.
dahyunąm Phl. Vd. 5. 38.
dahyūnąm Phl. Vd. 5. 32.
dahyūm T. 5.
dahštarᵊm cf. *fra°*.
dā cf. *paiti-nidaðāiti* and *nidaðāṯ*.
dāiti N. 84, 105 (2). Cf. *frāšmō°*, *hu-frāšmō°* and *han.°*

44   *dāitīm — didrəzvō*

dāitīm N. 5 (2), 32.

dāitǰe N. 50.

dāite Phl. Vd. **8**. 8.

dāitya N. 52 ; ZPGl. 13. 12.

dāitya-pairišta Phl. Vd. **5.** 2
(v. l. °*šti*).

dāityā N. 8, 30.

dāityehe N. 17.

dāityō N. 107 (also in *vaðāityō*
N. 107).

dāityō-aēsmąn N. 103.

dāityō-gātuš N. 78, 79 (3.)

dāityō-draonaṅhas [*ča* N. 53.

dāityō-baoiðyō N. 103.

dāiđī N. 102 (3).

dāim cf. *frāšmō*°.

dāta N. 97 ; Phl. Vd. **2**. 19 ;
T. 120 ; Vij. p. 12 (2) ; VS.
Extr. 4. Cf. *mazda*°, *sti*°,
spəntō° and *han*°.

dātarə W. Yt. **21**. 1 ; Yt. **22**. 1,
39.

dātahe N. 2 ; VS. Extr. 3.

dātāi VS. Extr. 1. Cf. *haða*°.

dātāiš ZPGl. 14. 1.

dātā [*ča* N. 61.

dātāčaaēti N. 61 (v. l. °*te* read
dātā [*ča aēte*).

dātəm v. l. N. 12 ; Vij. p. 126 ;
VS. Extr. 2. Cf. *avō*° and
zrvō°.

dātəmas [*ča* cf. *ayaptō*° and *as-
pərəzō*°.

dātōiš T. 116.

dātō-vaṅhəm Yt. (Vtp.) **24.** 20.

dātå Yt. (Vtp.) **24.** 43.

dāθra N. 16.

dāθranąm N. 83.

dāθrahe Pars. p. 534.

dāθri N. 84.

dādarayō N. 96 (2).

dādarəsa Yt. **22**. 10 ; Yt. (Vtp.)
24. 57.

dādrājōiš N. 12.

dāṱ T. 115 ; ZPGl. 13. 6.

dāna cf. *paiti*°.

[*dānazvāzəm* N. 82 (v. l. °*va-
nəm*).

dānunąm N. 52.

dānuš A. 77.

dāma cf. *duš*°.

dāmanąm Pars. p. 534 ; Vij. p.
181 ; W. **4**. 2.

dāmīm Pars. p. 534.

dāmōiš N. 61.

dāmōhu W. **4**. 2.

dāmąn N. 47, 61 ; Vij. p. 54 ;
Yt. **22**. 9 ; Yt. (Vtp.) **24.** 43,
51, 56.

dāyata Phl. Vd. **5**. 2.

dāyāṱ Yt. **22**. 2 ; Yt. (Vtp.) **24.**
53.

dāra ZPGl. 16. 9.

dārayəntəm cf. *vī*°.

dārayeite W. **4**. 3.

dārəm N. 84.

dāstra N. 67.

dāšta ZPGl. 27. 3.

dāštō-ratō T. 72.

diṱ A. 77, 78, 79, 80, 81.

didārəmnō cf. *vī*°.

didrəzvō T. 90, 91.

diδaēm Yt. (Vtp.) 24. 43.
dinānō N. 100.
dim AG. 10; N. 16, 39 (2),
  46, 67, 68; Pars. p. 534;
  Phl. Vd. 2. 5, 32; 7. 52; 8.
  8; T. 65, 116; W. 8. 1;
  Yt. 22. 9; Yt. (Vtp.) 24. 21,
  35, 55, 56, 63. Cf. *ā*°.
diš N. 38 (2).
dišanaya Yt. (Vtp.) 24. 51.
dišta ZPGl. 41. 2.
dišyatu Yt. (Vtp.) 24. 33.
dižaṯ T. 37.
dī Dk. (PSj.) 3. 131.
dīnā W. 9. 1 (read *daēna*).
dīš Yt. (Vtp.) 24. 30.
dī-šātōiš Dk. (P. Sj.) 3. 131.
duɣδa ZPGl. 5. 6.
duɣδovąm HtN. p. 483.
[*duɣδōvama*] v. l. HtN. p.
  483. (D.)
duɣδrąm Vij. p. 24.
duδuwibuzda ZPGl. 34. 5.
dunma ZPGl. 16. 8.
duye Vij. p. 87, 132.
dušitā [*čā* T. 6.
duškərəta Yt. (Vtp.) 24. 49.
dušxratum A. 81.
dušxraθwā Vij. p. 5.
dušdāma ZPGl. 27. 5.
duš [*čā* Phl. Vd. 3. 14; T. 38.
dušmainyavanąm Yt. (Vtp.) 24.
  25.
dušmainyuš Yt. (Vtp.) 24. 6.
dušmainyū-jayantəm Yt. (APZ.)
  23. 7.

dušmata Ganj. 5, 6 (2), 129;
  W. 3. 1, 2. Cf. *frāyō*°.
dušmataēibyas [*ča* W. Yt. 21. 17.
dušmata [*ča* W. Yt. 21. 7, 9, 11,
  13, 15.
dušmatəm [*ča* Phl. Vd. 7. 52.
dušmananhō Yt. 22. 36.
dušsastiš ZPGl. 27. 4.
dušsravaṅhe ZPGl. 27. 4.
duš-škyaoθnahe Yt. 22. 36.
duš-hąm-sāstayāi Yt. 22. 36.
dušxᵛarənå Yt. (Vtp.) 24. 43.
dužaṅhavō T. 17.
dužāθrəm A. 53.
dužāθrəm [*ča* N. 47.
dužūxta Ganj. 5, 6 (2), 129; W.
  3. 1, 2. Cf. *frāyō*ᶜ.
dužūxtaēibyas [*ča* W. Yt. 21. 17.
dužūxta [*ča* W. Yt. 21. 7, 9, 11,
  13, 15.
dužūxtayāi Yt. 22. 36.
dužgaintitarō Yt. 22. 25.
dužgaintitəməm Yt. 22. 26.
dužgaintiš Yt. 22. 25.
duždaēnahe Yt. 22. 36.
duždaēnō W. 4. 2.
duždå W. 8. 1.
duždåṅhō A. 19, 56.
dužvaćaṅhō Yt. 22. 36.
dužvarənāiš N. 35.
dužvaršta Ganj. 5, 6 (2), 129;
  W. 3. 1, 2. Cf. *frājō*°.
dužvaštaēibyas [*ča* W. Yt. 21.
  17.
dužvaršta [*ča* W. Yt. 21. 7, 9,
  11, 13, 15.

dužvarštayāi Yt. **22**. 36.

dužzaotārō Yt. (Vtp.) **24**. 12 (2).

dūm N. 59.

dūraēparayå A. 66.

dūraē-pārạm Yt. (APZ.) **23**. 4.

dūraē-srūtəm Yt. (Vtp.) **24**. 42.

dūrāaṯ [*ča* Yt. **22**. 13; Yt. (Vtp.) **24**. 59.

dūrāṯ Yt. (Vtp.) **24**. 51, 52.

dūre-paitinạm Yt. (Vtp.) **24**. 2.

dədanō N. 101.

dəṯ (or *bəṯ*) T. 68.

dənānō N. 100 (2), 101.

dənārō N. 90.

dəm N. 19; Yt. **22**. 17, 35, 37 (v. l. *dim*, Haug); Yt. (Vtp.) **24**. 47 (read *dim*).

dəmānəm T. 5.

dəmạnō-paθni ZPGl. 5. 2.

dərəgubyō W. **9**. 2.

dərətō ZPGl. 9. 3.

dərənǰyeiti N. 11.

dərəsavantəm cf. *afra*°.

dəuš N. 106.

dəuš-dātayå A. 56.

dōiəsnaθənti W. **8**. 2.

dōiθra ZPGl. 7. 13.   Cf. *vouru*°.

då Phl. Ys. **27** end, cf. *x°arənaz*°.

dåṇhō cf. *hu*°.

dạdrạxti Phl. Vd. **4**. 10.

dạm cf. *uši*°.

dạma Yt. (Vtp.) **24**. 20, 21.

dạmanạm Pars. p. 535.

dạmnsāvyạm FD. 7.

dạsuš cf. *karətō*°.

dạžðrəm N. 11.

dạhištāi N. 80.

dtarō N. 101 (read *tarō*).

[*dya*] v. l. FD. 6.

dyaēti cf. *paiti*°.

draoǰinō-bərətås [*ča* T. 36.

draoǰyehe N. 69.

draonaṇhas [*ča* cf. *aðāityō*° and *dāityō*°.

draonaṇhō N. 17.

draonibya N. 107.

draonō N. 17, 52, 53.   Cf. *dar*° and *fraðå*°.

draonå N. 30.

draos cf. *darəši*°.

draoš N. 100.

draǰō cf. *vitasti*°.

draǰōyeitīm T. 66.

dravatạm Phl. Vd. **19**. 30.

draǰe N. 42.

draǰō N. 11, 42 (2), 43, 44, 69 (2), 70, 83, 109; Phl. Vd. **9**. 32; **19**. 21; ZPGl. 16. 3; 29. 5. Cf. *čarətu*°, *frārāθni*° and *yārə*°.

drāǰaṇha N. 90.

drāǰaṇhō N. 103.

drigaove Dk. (P. Sj.) 3. 156.

driɣōš T. 100.

drīvīm [*ča* T. 47.

druxtō W. **9**. 1.

druxš W. **8**. 2 (2).

druɣīm [*ča* T. 47.

druǰa Yt. (Vtp.) **24**. 29.

drujaiti Phl. Vd. **4**. 10.

drujaskanąm Yt. (Vtp.) **24**. 26.

drujim ZPGl. 14. 7.

drujəm T. 41.

drujō W. **8**. 1 ; Yt. **22**. 34 ; Yt. (Vtp.) **24**. 25, 35.

druyanti N. 84 (read *druj°*).

družaite N. 84.

[*družahe*] v. l. N. 84.

drūjō W. **8**. 2.

drəgvatō T. 4, 84.

drənjayāaṯ[*ča* N. 11.

drvaite T. 110, 112 ; Yt. (Vtp.) **24**. 27.

drvaityāi Yt. **22**. 36.

drvatātəm Vij. p. 112 ; ZPGl. 11. 7.

drvatō N. 47, 54; Pars. p. 534 ; Phl. Ys. **67**. 51 (Sp.); Yt. **22**. 25, 26, 27–33.

drvatąm Pars. p. 535 ; Yt. (Vtp.) **24**. 26, 37.

drvantąm Vth. 19.

drvantō A. 19, 56.

drvō Yt. **22**. 34 (2) ; Yt. (Vtp.) **24**. 50 (2), 51.

drvā° A. 82 (3); T. 112 ; Yt. **22**. 19.

dva T. 99; Vij. p. 139 ; ZPGl. 1. 4.

dvaēibya N. 65.

dvaēšay- cf. *paiti°*.

dva[*ča* ZPGl. 41. 6.

dvadasa Vij. p. 179.

dvadasan-hāθrəm ZPGl. 43. 1.

dvayå ZPGl. 1. 5.

dvaraiti cf. *han°*.

dvarə Yt. (Vtp.) **24**. 36.

dvå N. 65.

t̰.

ṯkaēša Vth. 13, cf. *anya°*, *anyō°*, *arš°*, and *ašō°*.

ṯkaēšahe ZPGl. 43. 6.

ṯkaēšəm AG. 10.

ṯkaēšō ZPGl. 17. 8, 9.

ṯbaēšō Yt. (Vtp.) **24**. 37.

ṯbaēšå ZPGl. 28. 1.

ṯbiš- cf. *aṯbištō*.

ṯbišaētąm Yt. (Vtp.) **24**. 19.

ṯbišanuha Phl. Vd. **7**. 52.

ṯbišayantąm Yt. (Vtp.) **24**. 25 (2).

ṯbišiš Phl. Vd. **18**. 4.

ṯbištå Yt. (Vtp.) **24**. 51.

p.

pai . . . . . *asənti* N. 71.

paii N. 86 (read *paiti*).

paiō ZPGl. 24. 5.

paitanəm[*ča* Vij. p. 181.

paiti A. 17 (2); N. 2 (2), 7, 15, 17 (2), 20, 28 (2), 44, 45, 46 (2), 51, 54 (2), 55, 58, 60, 65 (2), 67, 68, 69 (6), 70 (7), 73, 74, 83, 84 (2), 88, 91, 96, 100 (2), 101, 103 (4), 106, 108 ; Phl. Vd. **2**. 5 ; **7**. 52 ; **17**. 9, 11 ; T.

8, 9, 33, 34, 45 (2), 47, 55,
79, 80, 81, 90, 91 ; Vij. p.
24, 128, 184 ; V̥th. 6 ; W.
4. 3 ; 9. 1 ; W. Yt. 21. 1 ;
Yt. 22. 7, 15 (3), 25, 38 (2);
Yt. (Vtp.) 24. 9, 19, 21, 26,
30, 50, 51, 54, 61 (2); ZPGl.
7. 1. 3 ; 13. 9. Cf. *daṅhu°*,
nmanō°, *vīs°* and *zantu°*.

paiti-aoxta Yt. 22. 11 ; Yt.
(Vtp.) 24. 1, 6, 8, 10, 12, 28,
34, 37, 40, 43, 58.

paiti-arå̃nti W. 4. 3.

paiti-asti [*ča* N. 22.

paitiastō ZPGl. 9. 8.

paiti-āpəm N. 70.

paiti-irite Yt. (Vtp.) 24. 15.

paiti-irista Ep. M. 1. 4. 3.

paiti-iristəm Ep. M. 1. 4. 3.

paitiəte ZPGl. 24. 10.

paiti [*ča* N. 64.

paiti-jaitīm Yt. (Vtp.) 24. 25.

paitijaθnō Yt. (Vtp.) 24. 17.

paitinəm Vij. p. 181.

paiti-jaṅhōiṯ N. 81.

paititim cf. *aiθra°* and *aēθ°*

paititəm Phl. Vd. 7. 52 (2).

paiti-dayō Phl. Vd. 1. 14.

paiti-dānahe Vij. p. 138.

paiti-dyaēti Vij. p. 24.

paiti-dvaēšayanta [*ča* Yt. 22. 11 ;
Yt. (Vtp.) 24. 58.

paitibaraiti N. 69.

paitibarāṯ N. 66, 67, 103.

paitibarō N. 67, 106.

paiti-narōiṯ N. 65 (read *bar°*).

paitinąm cf. *dūre°*.

paitim No. 67.

paiti-mruyå̃ Yt. (Vtp.) 24. 25.

paiti-raēčyāṯ Vij. p. 23.

paiti-vīrəm W. Yt. 21. 14.

paitiš N. 26 ; Vij. p. 160.

paitišantəm Yt. (Vtp.) 24. 52.

paitišāθrå̃ ZPGl. 15. 5.

paiti-šč W. Yt. 21. 2, 7, 9, 11,
13, 15, 17 ; Yt. 22. 40.

paitišta N. 83.

paitištanti N. 25.

paitištāna ZPGl. 11. 3.

paitišmarəntəm Yt.(Vtp.) 24. 52.

paitišmārənte Yt. (Vtp.) 24. 52.

paitiš-hahya AG. 7.

paitizaintyas [*ča* T. 89.

paiti-harəzāṯ N. 75.

paitī ZPGl. 24. 10.

paitīm FD. 7.

paitəšəntəm T. 15.

paitjuš N. 66.

paityahmi ZPGl. 12. 10.

paityāiti N. 11.

paityāδa ZPGl. 9. 8.

paityāpta N. 48. (Haug at
ZPGl. 76. 30, reads °*apta*.)

paityārəm Phl. Vd. 1. 1.

paityāstārəm [*ča* T. 30.

paityå̃nte T. 108.

paiθyå̃nte Yt. (Vtp.) 24. 28.

[*pai-barō*] v. l. N. 67 (read
paiti°).

pairāu N. 44.

pairi N. 7, 16, 17, 32 (3), 42,
46, 62, 95, 103 ; Phl. Vd.

4. 1, 10; Vij. p. 23, 145 (2), 151, 179; Vth. 3, 8; W. Yt. 21. 17; ZPGl. 17. 10.

pairiiriθyeiti Vij. p. 145 (2).

pairi-urusvaištiš N. 92.

pairiete ZPGl. 24. 7.

pairikanąm[*ča* ZPGl. 15. 12.

pairigayanti N. 80.

pairi-gərəmyāi N. 105.

pairijasāi N. 70.

pairiθwō A. 77, 78, 79, 80, 81. Cf. *a°*.

pairiyaoždāiti Vij. p. 148.

pairisačaiti N. 46, 47, 48, 49, 51.

pairištanhara N. 56.

pairištayeiti N. 44.

pairišti N. 103.

pairištəm Phl. Vd. 3. 42.

pairiš-hāvanayō Yt. (Vtp.) 24. 18.

pairyaoxta[*ča* T. 123.

pairyaštayeiti N. 44.

pairyeiti N. 42 (2).

pairyeitī N. 43.

pairyete ZPGl. 37. 5.

paurva ZPGl. 1. 4.

paurvāt̰ N. 37.

paē N. 57 (read *paēmainyāi*[*čit̰* D.).

paēma Yt. (Vtp.) 24. 50.

paēmanyō[*vā* Yt. (Vtp.) 24. 13.

paēmanyąm cf. *hačat̰°*.

paēmavaiti Yt. (Vtp.) 24. 49.

paēsa ZPGl. 24. 5.

paēsanh- cf. *stəhr°*.

paēsō cf. *vīspō°*.

paoiθya N. 29.

paoiri-fravaxšō N. 98.

paoiriš N. 98.

paoirīm Phl. Vd. 1. 1; Vij. p. 67, 128, 180; Yt. 22. 15; Yt. (Vtp.) 24. 44 (2), 61.

paoirya N. 102 (2).

paoiryanąm Pars. p. 534.

paoiryā Phl. Vd. 3. 14 (2) v. l. *°yāi*.

paoiryāi N. 105.

paoiryehe Phl. Vd. 2. 19.

paoiryō N. 2, 61, 71, 82; Vij. p. 53, 138; Yt. (Vtp.) 24. 23, 39.

paoiryō-t̰kaēša AG. 1.

paoiryąm N. 3; Yt. (Vtp.) 24. 54.

paouraya ZPGl. 7. 3.

paourīm ZPGl. 1. 4.

paouru Yt. (Vtp.) 24. 12.

paouru-gaonahe N. 65.

paouru-čarədayā̊ Māh Yt. 5.

paouru-fravāxšəm N. 98.

paouru-baēšazō Yt. (Vtp.) 24. 7.

paourum N. 44; Phl. Vd. 7. 52.

paouruvainīš[*ča* Yt. (Vtp.) 24. 29.

paouruša-gaonəm ZPGl. 6. 8.

paouru-x°arənanha Yt. (Vtp.) 24. 24.

paourvatātəm Yt. (Vtp.) 24. 6.

paourvaēibyō Vij. p. 126.

paōurunąm N. 13.

paōuruš T. 101.

paourvō N. 85 ; T. 68 ; Yt. (Vtp.) **24**. 26.

paoš ZPGl. 24. 9.

paðiryehe T. 7.

paðišəštem [*ča* T. 93.

pataiti cf. *hąm°*.

pataθa N. 83.

patarō Phl. Vd. **7**. 72.

patuš N. 57.

patənta ZPGl. 16. 4.

paθa N. 9. Cf. *vīspō°*.

paθanayå A. 66.

paθanō Vij. p. 145.

paθayeiti N. 105 (2).

paθayå N. 47 ; W. **5**. 1.

paθō ZPGl. 24. 8.

paθå Yt. (Vtp.) **24**. 54.

paθąm N. 47 ; W. **5**. 2.

paθwa N. 63.

paθni- cf. *dəmanō°* and *nmānō°*.

paθyeiti cf. *hąm°*.

padāiš N. 70.

padəm ZPGl. 41. 1.

pafraēta ZPGl. 40. 3.

pantanhəm ZPGl. 1. 7. °*im* (R.).

panča N. 42 ; Phl. Vd. **1**. 3 ; **2**. 41 ; **15**. 10 ; Vij. p. 184.

panča-dasa Phl. Vd. **8**. 100 ; **9**. 32 (2) ; ZPGl. 39. 6.

panča-dasanhō Vij. p. 157.

pan [*ča*] *dayasaya* N. 7.

panča-dasayå Yt. **22**. 9 ; Yt. (Vtp.) **24**. 56.

panča-sata ZPGl. 24. 6.

pančā [*ča* A. G. 5, 7, 19.

pančō Vij. p. 191.

panti N. 34.

pantəm cf. *aša°*.

pantå A. 77, 78, 79, 80, 81 ; HtN. p. 484.

pantąm Yt. **22**. 17, 35 ; Yt. (Vtp.) **24**. 42 (2), 63.

payanha [*ča* N. 59.

payanhō N. 30, 59 (2), 67.

payanhąm N. 66, 67 (2).

payå N. 67.

para N. 2 (3), 4, 8, 9, 11, 46, 48, 50 (2), 63 ; T. 71, 87 ; Vij. p. 5 (2) ; Yt. (Vtp.) **24**. 41, 44 (2), 50.

parairiθyeiti Yt. **22**. 1.

parairiθyō Yt. **22**. 16 (2).

parairistīm A. 19 ; Yt. **22** 18 (2) ; Yt. (Vtp.) **24**. 64 (2).

para [*ča* N. 4.

paračarantąm Vij. p. 133.

paradatanąm Vij. p. 54.

paranhačaiti N. 6.

paranhačaite N. 9, 10.

paranhačāi N. 7.

paranhačāiti N. 9.

paranhačāite N. 6.

paranhāiti N. 6.

parayaṯ N. 4. (v. l. in N. 3 according to MS. **TD**.).

parayanti N. 96.

parayāṯ N. 4, 5 (2), 80.

parayeiti N. 7.

parayeite N. 7.

parā Phl. Vd. **3**. 42.

parāiti N. 4, 83.

parā[ča N. 68 ; ZPGl. 6. 4.
parājītīm HtN. p. 484.
parāta ZPGl. 24. 3.
parāyaiti N. 2.
parāyāṯ N. 5 (2).
pari N. 103.
parəiti N. 13.
parətō-tanunąm N. 42.
parənti N. 13.
parəyeiti N. 41.
parō A. 41; HtN. p. 485 ; N.
    29, 32, 101; SlS. 13. 43 ; Yt.
    (Vtp.) 24. 49 (2), 51; ZPGl.
    9. 11.
parō-asti W. Yt. 21. 5.
parō-darš Yt. 22. 41.
paråntya ZPGl. 8. 2.
parvō Yt. (Vtp.) 24. 40.
paršta cf. zaini° and hąm°.
paršva ZPGl. 19. 1.
pasānō ZPGl. 10. 10.
pasu Dk. (P. Sj.) 3. 131 ; N. 83.
pasuyəbīš N. 57.
pasu-vastranąm[ča N. 58.
pasu-vastrahe ZPGl. 6. 9.
pasuš N. 58.
pasu-šurvąn ZPGl. 40. 1.
pasuš[ča N. 56.
pasuš-xᵛarəθəm Phl. Vd. 19. 41.
pasūm N. 58, 67 (2) ; Yt. (Vtp.)
    24. 44.
pasō N. 63.
paskāṯ Yt. 22. 14 ; Yt. (Vtp.)
    24. 60.
pasča A. 19 ; N. 7 (2), 32, 48,
    58, 87, 95, 103 ; Vij. p. 127,

138, 179 (2) ; W. Yt. 21. 9 ;
    Yt. 22. 18 (2), 36 (2) ; Yt.
    (APZ.) 23. 8 ; Yt. (Vtp.) 24.
    5, 29, 64 (3) ; ZPGl. 9. 12 ;
    10. 1.
pasčaita N. 4, 46, 50.
pasčaiti N. 9 (2), 11, 14, 42 ;
    Vij. p. 88, 89, 139, 158, 160,
    181, 188:
pasčaite Vij. p. 128.
pasčaēta v. l. N. 4 ; Phl. Vd.
    2. 5, 19 ; T. 39, 82.
pasčič N. 20.   Avestan?
pasčiti Vij. p. 179.
pasvarəzdəs[ča N. 97.
pasvā N. 65.
pasvō N. 65 ; ZPGl. 39. 7.
pašąai Phl. Ys. 38. 7 (Sp.).   Is
    this Avestan?
pašnəm ZPGl. 8. 1.
pāiti A. 77, 78, 79, 80 ; Vij. p.
    67.
pāityāi N. 71.
pāiði Phl. Vd. 7. 43.
pāipiθvąm N. 64.
[pāiptvąm] v. l. N. 64.
pāiri ZPGl. 9. 13.
pāta ZPGl. 24. 4.
pātayas[ča Yt. (Vtp.) 24. 43.
pātayāi cf. ni°.
pāθå N. 29.
pāða ZPGl. 24. 4.
pāðauē Phl. Ys. 64. 48 (Sp.).
pāðanuhantəm ZPGl. 40. 1.
pānčāstəm ZPGl. 24. 6 (R. reads
    pančasatəm).

pāntəm cf. aša°.

pāpayamnō T. 34.

pāpiθwa N. 62.

pāpiθwąm N. 64 (2).

pāyūm Vij. p. 54.

pār- cf. duraē°.

pārantarəm N. 12.

pārandi [ča Yt. (Vtp.) 24. 8.

pārayaṯ N. 3 (MS. TD. par°).

pārayantu CB. (2).

pārayāṯ N. 1.

pārəm ZPGl. 24. 7 ; 40. 3.

pārəṣ̌manāi N. 84.

pāšnābyō Phl. Vd. 2. 32.

piti Vij. p. 99.

pitum ZPGl. 24. 5.

pitūm CB. (2).

pitō Vij. p. 145.

piθw- cf. tanro° and tarō°

pipyūšinąm cf. a°.

piryeiti cf. fra°.

pišo-tanuš N. 44.   Cf. pəsō°.

pīsa T. 90, 91.

puxða N. 102 ; Vij. p. 138, 139 ; ZPGl. 1. 7 ; 24. 6.

puxðəm N. 67 (2), 82 ; Vij. p. 138.

puθra Vij. p. 99, 158 ; Vth. 4, 5, 9, 16 ; Yt. (APZ.) 23. 1, 5 ; Yt. (Vtp.) 24. 1 (2), 3, 6, 8, 9, 10, 11, 12, 19, 24, 26, 28, 37, 40, 43, 53, 54, 65 ; ZPGl. 15. 8.   Cf. a°.

puθranąm N. 52.

puθrahe FD. 7 ; N. 54 ; Yt. (Vtp.) 24. 49.

puθrəm FD. 7 ; Phl. Vd. 12. 4 ; Vij. p. 24, 25 ; Yt. (Vtp.) 24. 26.

puθrō Vij. p. 25 ; Yt. (Vtp.) 24. 1, 3, 21, 22, 31, 33, 37, 45, 52 ; ZPGl. 16. 11.

puθrąm Vij. p. 179 ; Yt. (Vtp.) 24. 26.   Cf. hačaṯ°.

puθrąs Yt. (Vtp.) 24. 34, 46.

puyąn cf. a°.

pusąm ZPGl. 24. 10.

pūiti Phl. Vd. 7. 43.

pərəgərəptayāṯ Vth. 18.

pərətuš ZPGl. 24. 3.

pərətūm T. 2 ; Vij. p. 25.   Cf. činvaṯ°.

pərətō-tanunąm Phl. Vd. 7. 52.

pərəθa cf. tanu°.

[pərənahe] v. l. Phl. Vd. 8. 22.

pərənāi ZPGl. 24. 4.

pərənāiu ZPGl. 24. 4.

pərənāyu ZPGl. 4. 5.

pərənāyunąm ZPGl. 4. 6. Cf. a°.

pərənāyuš ZPGl. 4. 5.

pərənāyū cf. a°.

pərənāvayå ZPGl. 24. 9.

pərənəm Phl. Vd. 8. 22 ; ZPGl. 24. 3.

pərəmnāi ZPGl. 13. 9.

pərəsaṯ Vij. p. 53 ; Vth. 1 ; W. Yt. 21. 1 ; Yt. 22. 1, 19 ; Yt. (Vtp.) 24. 21.

pərəsahi Yt. 22. 17, 35 ; Yt. (Vtp.) 24. 63.

pərəsahe Phl. Vd. 7. 52.

pərəsā Phl. Vd. **19.** 10 ; ZPGl.
.14. 10.

pərəsāṯ Yt. (Vtp.) **24.** 41.

pərəsu ZPGl. 10. 9.

pərəsənti N. 61.

pərəsō N. 58 ; Yt. **22.** 10, 16,
17, 34, 35 ; Yt. (Vtp.) **24.**
33, 55, 57, 62, 63.

pərəsånte Yt. (Vtp.) **24.** 40.

pərəsmanaēšu[*ča* Yt. (Vtp.) **24.**
36.

pəsånte T. 100.

pəšūm Yt. (Vtp.) **24.** 42.

pəšo-tanuš ZPGl. 24. 8.

pəsō-tanuš Yt. (Vtp.) **24.** 4 ;
ZPGl. 37. 4.

pəšō-tanvaṯ Vth. 12.

pəšō-tanve Phl. Vd. **7.** 52.

pē N. 14.

pēvāčim N. 42.

pouru-aspəm Yt. (APZ.) **23.** 4.

pouru-aspō Yt. (Vtp.) **24.** 2.

pouru-gāvō Yt. (Vtp.) **24.** 2.

pouru-gō Yt. (APZ.) **23.** 4.

pouru[*čiṯ* N. 65.

pouru-ǰirō Yt. (APZ.) **23.** 2.

pouru-mahrkō Yt. (Vtp.) **24.** 43.

pouruyō ZPGl. 17. 2.

pouru-spaxštīm Yt.(Vtp.)**24.** 25.

[*pourušaspahe*] v. l. F. D. 4.

pourušaspahe Yt. (Vtp.) **24.** 2.

pourušaspəm F. D. 4; Yt.(APZ.)
23. 4.

pourušaspō ZPGl. 15. 8.

pouru-x͏ᵛarənanhō Phl. Vd. **5.**
9 ; Yt. (Vtp.) **24.** 7.

pouru-x͏ᵛāθrəm Yt. (APZ.) 23. 7.

pourvō Yt. **22.** 16, 34 ; Yt.
(Vtp.) **24.** 62.

pōiθwəm Yt. (Vtp.) **24.** 9.

pōiṯ N. 71.

pōisāiṯ N. 109. Cf. *u°* ?

pōuru-mahrkō A. 28.

pąntå FD. 2.

pąm ZPGl. 32. 6.

pąsanuš ZPGl. 24. 8.

pąstahe ZPGl. 6. 9.

pąsnuš A. 84 (3).

ptaṯ ZPGl. 24. 9.

ptarənta N. 51.

pfre T. 25 (D. adds read *pafre*).

[*prā*[*ča*] v. l. N. 68. Cf. *par°*.

f.

fəðri ZPGl. 26. 9.

fərəθwəm cf. *hu°*.

fr N. 46 (read *frayāraṯ*).

fra A. 77 ; Phl. Vd. **3.** 14 ; T.
36.

fraiar ZPGl. 42. 4.

frauąxš ZPGl. 10. 5.

fraurvaixti N. 84.

fraurvaērxte N. 84.

fraurvaēsyō N. 59.

fraēazaite ZPGl. 15. 4 (read
fravazaite ?)

fraēšta A. 56 ; ZPGl. 26. 11.

fraēšyāmahe T. 71.

fraoirišaiti W. Yt. **21.** 17.

fraoxtō W. Yt. **21.** 4.

fraorət T. 62.

fraorət-fraxšni W. Yt. 21. 3.

fraðiritarāt̰ N. 58.

frakairi Phl. Vd. 9. 294.

frakaire Phl. Vd. 19. 41.

frakārayeiti N. 101.

frakārayōiš ZPGl. 18. 8.

frakinəm A. 66.

frakəm N. 74.

frakərənaot̰ Phl. Vd. 8. 103 ; 19. 41.

frakərənavintąm Vij. p. 128.

frakərənōit̰ Vij. p. 148.

frakərəntənti Vij. p. 136.

fraxni T. 62 (read *fraxšnı*).

fraxšti Yt. 22. 37.

fraxšni cf. *fraorət̰°*.

fragatōit̰ ZPGl. 42. 11. Cf. *raočaṅhąm°*.

fragōurvayāt̰ Vij. p. 145.

fraɣrāɣrāyeiti N. 19.

fraɣrārayō N. 19.

fraɣrisəmnō W. Yt. 21. 13.

fračarātō N. 103.

fračarənti N. 53.

frajasaiti N. 46, 47, 48, 49, 50, 51, 104.

frajasāiti Vij. p. 148, 160.

frajasāt̰ Vij. p. 24.

frajasōit̰ Vij. p. 158 (2).

frataire Yt. 22. 14 ; Yt. (Vtp.) 24. 60.

frataurunås̰ [*ča* N. 40.

fratat̰ N.'66.

fratarənixma Yt. (Vtp.) 24. 43.

fratarəm Yt. (Vtp.) 24. 29.

fratarōtare Yt. 22. 14 ; Yt. (Vtp.) 24. 60.

fratarąn N. 79.

fratarąm N. 79 (2).

fratufriš N. 100.

fratufrya N. 24.

fratəməm Phl. Vd. 18. 43.

fratəməm [*ča* Vij. p. 128.

fratərəsaiti A. 19 ; Yt. (Vtp.) 24. 27.

fratərəsənti A. 19 ; Yt. (Vtp.) 24. 27.

fraθaṅha N. 90.

fraθaṅhəm cf. *baē-ərəzu°*.

fraθō N. 70.

fraθwaršta W. 1. 2.

fraθyehe N. 69.

fraθrāθvayō N. 104.

fradaxštanąm T. 34.

fradaθāi N. 103 ; Pars. p. 535 (5) ; ZPGl. 26. 9.

fradaθəm W. 9. 2 ; Yt. (Vtp.) 24. 39 ; ZPGl. 13. 3.

fradaθąm W. 4. 1.

fradaðāiti Vij. p. 138, 139, 158.

fradaðāt̰ Vij. p. 25, 181.

fradarayōit̰ N. 67.

fradarišta [*čit̰* N. 67.

fradahštarəm [*čā* T. 30 (*dax°*.)

fradərəsavantəm cf. *a°*.

fradvaraiti Yt. 22. 42.

fraðāitīm N. 53.

fraðå-draonō N. 30.

frapa N. 54.

frapiryeiti Phl. Vd. 5. 9.

frafrā T. 2.

frabaraite N. 48.

frabaraṯ Yt. 22. 15 (4), 27–33 ; Yt. (Vtp.) 24. 61 (2).

frabaravaṯ N. 71.

frabarāṯ Vij. p. 24.

frabarəta N. 67, 71.

frabarətaš Yt. (Vtp.) 24. 15.

frabarətārəm N. 82.

frabarōiṯ N. 68 ; Phl. Vd. 3. 14 (v. l. °ōiš) ; Vij. p. 128.

frabarōiš Vij. p. 139.

[*frabiθyamnō*] v. l. W. Yt. 21. 28 (Haug). Read *frabuδyamnō?*

frabərəta N. 68.

frabərətarš N. 74, 79, 81.

frabda ZPGl. 11. 4.

franuharəiti W. Yt. 21. 9.

franuharəta W. Yt. 21. 7.

franharəzaiti Vth. 3, 8.

franharəzōiṯ N. 11.

franharōiṯ N. 71.

franhərəzaṯ Phl. Vd. 2. 5.

franata N. 65.

franuδyamnō W. Yt. 21. 13.

framanīm T. 96.

framaraiti N. 21, 38, 42.

framarənti N. 23, 52.

framarəntəm N. 21, 52.

framarəmnō N. 26.

framavainti N. 60.

framərətahe T. 106.

framərənti N. 39.

framərəzaiti Phl. Vd. 7. 52.

framraomi W. 4. 2.

framraōmi T. 66.

framravātō W. 9. 1.

framravānō W. 9. 1.

framruyå Yt. (Vtp.) 24. 26, 35.

framrvānā Phl. Vd. 4. 1.

framrvąnō W. Yt. 21. 4.

frayaēre N. 53.

frayaδjaiti ZPGl. 35. 7.

frayaṯ N. 103.

frayaṅhąm N. 65.

frayarāi N. 47.

frayarəna N. 9.

frayare ZPGl. 26. 10.

frayazāiti N. 81.

frayō-huxtayāi Yt. (Vtp.) 24. 64 (2).

frayō-hvarštayāi Yt. (Vtp.) 24. 64 (2).

frayąhaθawδ[*ča* Yt. (Vtp.) 24. 34 (v. l. *fryąnhaxaθwaδa-*[*ča*).

fravaiti N. 17.

fravaityanąm N. 54.

fravairi Phl. Vd. 8. 103 (v. l. *frak°*).

fravaočāi Yt. (Vtp.) 24. 22.

fravaočāṯ Yt. (Vtp.) 24. 20.

fravaočāma Yt. (Vtp.) 24. 13, 20, 34, 65.

fravaočāmi Yt. (Vtp.) 24. 46, 52.

fravakāi Yt. 22. 38.

fravačaṯ Vij. p. 126.

fravatim[*ča* N. 65.

fravarane Phl. Vd. 9. 32, 57 ; 19. 2.

fravarāne Māh. Yt. 0 ; N. 20

(2), 37, 58, 61 (7), 67 ; Pars.
p. 521 ; PI ; SlS. **13**. 1 ; Vij.
p. 97, 164, 165 ; W. **2**. 1 ;
6. 2.

fravarānē Phl. Ys. **27** end ; **61**
end (Sp.).

fravarəta Yt. **22**. 37.

fravašayō CB ; W. **1**. 2 ; Yt.
22. 39.

fravašāimnō N. 37 (*fra vā*
šāimnō).

fravašiš [*ča* N. 70.

fravašīm Phl. Vd. **2**. 5 ; Yt. **22**.
37.

fravašə̄e N. 46 ; Vij. p. 128 ;
W. **2**. 1, 3.

fravašyō Vij. p. 156.

fravākəm W. Yt. **21**. 1.

fravāxš ZPGl. 11. 1.

fravāxšō N. 98.   Cf. *paouru°*.

fravāxšnaēibya N. 107.

fravāxšyanąm N. 105.

frasasta ZPGl. **26**. 10.

frasastayaē [*ča* N. 46 (3), 48,
61, 81 ; Pars. p. 521 (2);
SlS. **13**. 1 ; W. **2**. 1.

frasastaya [*ča* Vij. p. 164.

frasastayāṯ Vij. p. 145.

frastaraityō N. 102.

frastarətəm Yt. (Vtp.) **24**. 23.

frastarənaēta N. 89.

frastarənti N. 60, 89, 97, 98
(2), 101 (2), 104.

frastavanō W. Yt. **21**. 7, 9, 11,
13, 15.

frastuye N. 20, 37, 46 (2);

Pars. p. 521 ; SlS. **13**. 1 ;
Vij. p. 151.

frastərənāiti N. 70.

frastərənti N. 60.

fraspayōiš A. 28.

frasnayāiti Vij. p. 89.

frasnayehi Yt. (Vtp.) **24**. 49.

frasrāvayamnahe N. 20.

frasrāvayāiti N. 33, 72.

frasrāvayeiti N. 50.

frasrāvayō N. 16.

frasrāvayōiṯ N. 81 ; Vij. p. 181.

frasravaynti Vij. 139.

frasruiti N. 7.

frasrūtå N. 70.

frasråšyehe N. 20.

fraša N. 71.

frašaoštra Yt. (Vtp.) **24**. 11, 54,
55.

frašaoštraēibya Yt. (Vtp.) **24**. 11.

frašaoštrō N. 63.

fraša-kərəti Ganj. 1, 101, 102,
103.

frašāvayō N. 103.

frašumaitīš T. 124.

frašusaiti Phl. Vd. **18**. 14.

frašūitiš N. 103.

frašūtōiṯ T. 39.

frašūsaitē Phl. Ys. **56**. 1 (Sp.).

frašō-čarəθrå A. 69.

frašōtəməm Pars. p. 521; W. **9**.
2.

frašōšō-mąθrahe N. 22.

frašnəm ZPGl. 10. 12.

frazainti A. 48.

frazaintivaiti Yt. (Vtp.) **24**. 49.

frazaintīm Vij. p. 158.

frazānaiti ZPGl. 17. 10.

frazušō N. 92.

frazdānaom ZPGl. 17. 3.

frahančintarə N. 68.

frā N. 48 (2), 60, 61, 71, 103 ; T. 29 ; Vij. p. 165, 166 ; W. 1. 1 ; 7. 2 ; ZPGl. 14. 4.

frāite N. 50.

frāiziš N. 40.

fraurusti N. 2.

frākərəitīm HtN. p. 484.

frākərəntaṭ A. 28.

frākərəstō A. 57.

frāxšašyanąm N. 105 (read *fravāxšyanąm*).

frātavaṭ Yt. (Vtp.) 24. 51.

frātiš N. 48.

frā-tē Yt. (Vtp.) 24. 49.

frādaṭ-gaēθəm N. 61.

frādaṭ-gaēθąm Yt. (Vtp.) 24. 14.

frāδati[ča Yt. (Vtp.) 24. 15.

frāδāiti T. 42.

frāpahe N. 47.

frā-nasūm Ep. M. 1. 4. 3.

frāma N. 19.

frāmā N. 20.

frāmrūiti N. 13.

frāyaṅhō T. 99.

frāyantō Yt. (Vtp.) 24. 42.

frāyaza Vij. p. 181.

frāyazaiti N. 81.

frāyazāne Yt. (Vtp.) 24. 20, 21.

frāyazāmaide N. 65.

frāyazånti Vij. p. 127.

frāyazyāṭ Vij. p. 136.

frāyu . . . təm N. 71.

frāyō-dušmatayāi Yt. 22. 36.

frāyō-vohunąm Yt. (Vtp.) 24. 35.

frāyō-huxtayāi Yt. 22. 18.

frāyō-humatayāi Yt. 22. 18 ; Yt. (Vtp.) 24. 64 (2).

frāyō-humatahe T. 89.

frāyō-humatō T. 23.

frāyō-hūxtahe T. 89.

frāyō-hūxtō T. 23.

frāyō-hvarəštahe T. 89.

frāyō-hvarštayāi Yt. 22. 18.

frāyō-hvarštō T. 23.

frāra N. 10 (2).

frārāiti T. 52.

frārāitīš[ča T. 77.

frārāθni-drājō Phl. Vd. 5. 4.

frāraiθya ZPGl. 13. 12.

frāraθne N. 103.

frārāiθyanąm T. 119.

frārāδān ZPGl. 10. 4.

frāšənti T. 100.

frāšmō-dāitīm N. 58. Cf. *hu°*.

frāšmō-dāitōe N. 51.

frāšmō-dāitōiṭ N. 48.

frāšmō-dāim N. 48.

fritōiš N. 19.

fritąm Yt. (Vtp.) 24. 60.

frityō cf. *a°*.

friθitəm cf. *ātarə°*.

friθōtarąm Yt. 22. 14.

friθąm Yt. 22. 14.

friδast N. 67.

frinayantəma N. 70.

frim ZPGl. 26. 9.

frīn- cf. *a°*.

frīm T. 22 ; Yt. (Vtp.) **24**. 51.

frənč- N. 97.

frəraiti cf. *a°*.

frərənaoṯ SlS. **11**. 6.

frən- N. 97.

frərətōiṯ Yt. **22**. 41.

frərənta Yt. **22**. 9.

frērənti Yt. (Vtp.) **24**. 56.

frōiṯ N. 6.

frōtāiš T. 2.

frąs ZPGl. 26. 10.

fryō T. 23.

fšu ZPGl. 19. 4.

fšuta ZPGl. 26. 11.

fšum cf. *maṯ°*.

fšuyantō Yt. (APZ.) **23**. 5 ; Yt. (Vtp.) **24**. 3, 16.

fšuyå cf. *ərədra°*.

fšuyąn Yt. (Vtp.) **24**. 46.

fštāna ZPGl. 10. 6.

fšny- cf. *ərədva°*.

fšyō ZPGl. 19. 4 ; 26. 11.

b.

bairaiti N. 60.

bairyeinte Yt. (Vtp.) **24**. 35 (2)

baē ZPGl. **28**. 1.

baē-ərəzu Phl. Vd. **18**. 2.

baē-ərəzu-fraθaṇhəm Phl. Vd. **18**. 1.

baēvarāi Yt. (Vtp.) **24**. 19.

baēvārə W. Yt. **21**. 5, 12.

baevarə-vaēδayanəm Yt. (Vtp.) **24**. 45.

baēvarōtəmō-baēvara Yt. (Vtp.) **24**. 19.

haēšaza ZPGl. **28**. 1.

baēšazəm W. **9**. 1, 2 ; Yt. (Vtp.) **24**. 39.

baēšazō cf. *paouru°*.

baēšazyō W. **9**. 1.

baoiδi N. 28 ; Yt. (Vtp.) **24**. 38. Cf. *hu°*.

baoiδīm N. 103 (2).

baoiδyeita[*ča* Vij. p. 158.

baoiδyō cf. *dāityō°*.

baoiδiš[*ča* Yt. **22**. 7.

baoišya[*ča* Yt. (Vtp.) **24**. 59.

baouruš[*ča* N. 91.

baoδajaṯ ZPGl. 32. 8.

baoδaṇhas[*ča* Yt. **22**. 17, 35 ; Yt. (Vtp.) **24**. 63.

baoδaṇhō ZPGl. **28**. 5.

baoδas[*ča* I. 71.

baoδəm A. 19 ; Yt. (Vtp.) **24**. 27.

baoδō N. 59 ; Yt. (Vtp.) **24**. 28, 51 ; ZPGl. **28**. 4.

baoδō-baxti[*ča* Yt. (Vtp.) **24**. 33.

baoδō-varšta W. **3**. 1 (2).

baoδō-varštahe Yt. (Vtp.) **24**. 44 (2) ; ZPGl 3. 3 ; 32. 8.

baosayā[*ča* Yt. (Vtp.) **24**. 37.

baosavas[*ča* Yt. **22**. 13.

baošəm ZPGl. **28**. 6.

baōyō N. 4.

baxəδrāi Yt. (Vtp.) **24**. 52.

baxta[*ča* Yt. (Vtp.) **24**. 38.

baxtəm cf. *daṅhu°*, *nmānō°*,
vīspe° and *zantu°*.
baxtō cf. *bāγō°*.
baxðra ZPGl. 28. 3.
baxšaṯ ZPGl. 13. 3.
baxšayata Yt. (Vtp.) 24. 8.
baxšayāaṯ[ča N. 76.
baxšå̆nti Yt. (Vtp.) 24. 34, 46.
baγa ZPGl. 28. 2.
baγəm Vij. p. 24 (3). Cf. *aēvō°*.
baγąm SlS. 13. 1.
baγąm[ča N. 47.
[*bajanaō*] v. l. N. 66.
bajinō N. 66, 67.
baðrō cf. *hu°*.
baṅha cf. *vī°*.
baṅhəm Yt. (Vtp.) 24. 26.
bantå̆ ZPGl. 28. 3.
bandəm Vij. p. 138.
bandå̆ ZPGl. 28. 3.
bandyāṯ Vij. p. 138.
bar- cf. *ava°*, *upa°*, *uz°*, *paiti°*,
fra°, niž°, vī° and *hąm°*.
bara N. 54, 105.
baraiti N. 60, 63 (2), 103 ; T.
43 ; Vij. p. 25.
baraite T. 81 ; ZPGl. 14. 6.
baraētā W. 9. 2.
barajāim[ča Yt. (Vtp.) 24. 40.
barata N. 103.
baraṯ Phl. Vd. 2. 10 ; Vij.p. 68.
barahe Yt. (Vtp.) 24. 50.
barāiti N. 69.
barātō N. 64 (4).
barāṯ N. 65, 74, 77 ; T. 36,
78, 80.

barāmi N. 48 ; W. 7. 2. Cf
usbī°.
barāhi Yt. (Vtp.) 24. 50.
barəta cf. *bərəta*.
[*barətanąm*] v. l. Yt. 22. 38
(Haug).
barətå̊s[ča cf. *draojinō°*.
barətąm ZPGl. 16. 8. Cf. *ava°*.
barəθra ZPGl. 28. 4.
barəθri ZPGl. 5. 3.
barənti N. 54, 95, 100 (2), 101,
103 ; Vij. p. 116.
barəntu CB.
barəmne T. 47.
barəmnō N. 37 ; T. 10.
barəs[ča N. 71, 98.
barəsma N. 46 (2), 69, 70 (3),
83, 89, 98, 99, 100, 101,
102, 104, 105 ; Yt. (Vtp.)
24. 23.
barəsmaine N. 69 (2).
barəsmaēne N. 97.
barəsma[ča N. 60 (2), 68.
barəsma[čiṯ N. 69.
barəsman N. 62.
barəsmana N. 90, 108 ; Vij. p.
152 ; Yt. (Vtp.) 24. 23.
barəsme N. 70.
barəsmō N. 103.
barəsmō-stərəiti T. 40.
barəsmąn N. 70 (4), 74, 79 (2),
97, 102, 103 (2).
barəšna Phl. Ys. 9. 35.
barəšnšō N. 65.
barəzimanąm N. 47.
barəzištəm N. 47.

barəzyō T. 41.

baroždahum ZPGl. 10. 9.

barō N. 11, 37, 98 (2), 99, 103, 104, 108; Phl. Vd. 5. 34; 6. 26.

barōiṭ N. 28, 67, 69 (2), 70 (7), 71.

barōiθrō-taēžim Phl. Vd. 18. 14.

barōiθrō-taēžəm Phl. Ys. 56. 1.

barånti N. 54.

baršnūm [*ča* Vij. p. 89.

bavaiti A. 53, 77, 78, 79, 80, 81; Phl. Vd. 13. 96 (Sp.); Vij. p. 24, 179 (2); Vth. 13; W. 8. 2.

bavainti Vth. 19.

bavatəm Phl. Vd. 7. 52.

bavaṭ N. 63; Phl. Vd. 2. 5; Yt. (Vtp.) 24. 10, 31, 34, 43, 46.

bavarə-mištəm Yt. (Vtp.) 24. 45.

bavāṭ N. 67; W. 4. 3; Yt. (Vtp.) 24. 4, 28, 44.

bavāni Yt. (Vtp.) 24. 38.

bavāhi Yt. (APZ.) 23. 2 (3), 3 (5), 4 (5); Yt. (Vtp.) 24. 4 (4), 5 (4), 6 (5), 7 (4).

bavå Yt. (Vtp.) 24. 8.

bavånti W. 4. 3.

bavąn Yt. (Vtp.) 24. 43.

baši ZPGl. 28. 6.

baši-drajanhō N. 108 v. l. *baiši°*.

bazda N. 56.

bā T. 55; W. Yt. 21. 7, 9 (2), 11 (2), 13 (2), 15 (2), 17;

Yt. 22. 11, 20; Yt. (Vtp.) 24. 54, 58.

bāɣō-baxtō Yt. (Vtp.) 24. 25.

bāδa N. 30; Vij. p. 180; Yt. (Vtp.) 24. 35, 36 (3), 53; ZPGl. 28. 2.

bāmanyå ZPGl. 18. 5 (R. reads *bāmanivå*).

bāmya ZPGl. 6. 3.

bāzava ZPGl. 10. 2.

bāzvō cf. *aurušaᵒ*.

bitim ZPGl. 1. 5.

bitīm N. 82; Phl. Vd. 1. 1; Yt. 22. 15; Yt. (Vtp.) 24. 61.

bityā N. 102 (2).

bityō N. 2, 37; Vij. p. 138; Yt. (Vtp.) 24. 23.

bityå N. 42.

bityąm Yt. 22. 3, 21; Yt. (Vtp.) 24. 54.

biθvehe T. 8.

bipiθwō SkN. p. 480; ZPGl. 38. 6.

bivakayehe Phl. Vd. 7. 43.

bis N. 86 (2).

bisarəm [*ča* T. 60.

bistaorəm N. 45.

biš N. 8, 31, 97. Cf. *hāθrakaēᵒ*.

biš-aētavaṭ ZPGl. 41. 8, 10.

bišiš-framātō ZPGl. 28. 5.

bišəš W. 9. 1.

bizangrəm Phl. Vd. 7. 52.

bī N. 48; W. 7. 2. Cf. *usbī-barāmi*.

bīraošaṭ T. 24 (D. conjectures *draošaṭ*).

bīšāmrūta N. 33, 35.
buiri Yt. (Vtp.) 24. 45 (4).
buxtā W. 2. 2.
buji ZPGl. 28. 6.
buδa Vth. 11.
bunāṯ A. 77.
bunəm A. 28 ; ZPGl. 12. 10.
bunjayāṯ A. 58.
buyāṯ CB (4) ; ZPGl. 28. 2.
buyāriš Yt. (Vtp.) 24. 7.
buyå Yt. (Vtp.) 24. 9 (2).
bušyąsta Yt. 22. 42.
buzinanąm [*ča* N. 67.
būjyamanō Vij. p. 160, 181.
būjyānəm Vij. p. 157.
bərəxδōtarąm Yt. 22. 14.
bərəxδąm Yt. 22. 14.
bərəji T. 106.
bərəjyąstəmō N. 1.
bəreite cf. *aēsmō°*.
bərəta N. 79.
bərətanąm Yt. 22. 18, 36 ; Yt.
    (Vtp.) 24. 64.
bərətayaē [*ča* cf. *upa°*.
bərətarš cf. *fra°*.
bərətābyō cf. *yasō°*.
bərətibyō cf. *vaxš°*.
bərətiš N. 2.   Cf. *ušta°, vanta°*
    and *hu°*.
bərətīm N. 2.
bərətəm N. 103.
bərəte cf. *araθwyō°*.
bərətō Phl. Vd. 3. 14.

bərətå ZPGl. 30. 8.   Cf. *zurō°*.
bərətås [*ča* cf. *draojinō°*.
bərətąm A. 16.
bərətyāṯ Yt. (Vtp.) 24. 25.
bərəθyāṯ Yt. (Vtp.) 24. 31,
    52.
bərəs cf. *ā°*.
bərəzaityå Yt. 22. 23 (Haug).
bərəzata ZPGl. 8. 10.
bərəzatō N. 47 (2), 48 (2) ; Phl.
    Ys. 22. 5 ; Vij. p. 105, 166
    (2) ; W. 7. 1, 2.
bərəzaṯ N. 61 (2) ; Yt. (Vtp.)
    24. 46.
bərəzaṯ-varəzi T. 73.
bərəzanąm cf. *nərə°*.
bərəzanti Vij. p. 50.
bərəzantyå Yt. (Vtp.) 24. 56.
bərəzi-stūnəm Yt. (Vtp.) 24. 9.
bərəzō N. 46.
bąθrō ZPGl. 28. 7.
bązō Phl. Vd. 2. 19.
bdātəm cf. *ana°*.
bdōištəm N. 9.
byaṅha ZPGl. 28. 4.
brāta Yt. (Vtp.) 24. 10.
brātravaitīš Yt. (Vtp.) 24. 36.
brāθranąm T. 96.
brāθrəm Yt. (Vtp.) 24. 10.
brənjayāiti N. 94 (D. suggests
    d°).
bvaṯ T. 92, 93 ; Yt. (Vtp.) 24.
    30, 31 ; ZPGl. 11. 11.

n.

na N. 92.
nairi N. 84.

nairīm [*ča* Yt. (Vtp.) 24. 40.
nairyō N. 5.

nairyō-saṇhahe N. 47.

naē[*ča* T. 39.

naē[*čiš* A. 58 ; FD. 3 ; W. 4. 2.

naēta T. 122.

naēða A. 66 ; Vij. p. 89 ; Yt. (Vtp.) 24. 35.

naēða[*ča* Yt. (Vtp.) 24. 15, 30.

naēṭa T. 117.

naēpatavaitīm cf. *haða°*.

naēm N. 44.

naēmaēibya Phl. Vd. 13. 34 (2), 85 (2) (Sp.), 102 (Sp.).

naēmaēibyō Yt. 22. 7, 25, 42.

naēmaṭ N. 11 (2), 37, 58, 60, 69 (2), 71, 79 (2), 93, 94, 99, 104 (2) ; T. 38 ; Yt. 22. 7, 25, 42.

naēmi-rāθa Vth. 16, 17.

naēməm N. 42, 44 (2), 45 ; Vij. p. 24.

naēmō N. 33, 64.

naēmąm ZPGl. 9. 13.

naēm[*ča* N. 11.

naēre ZPGl. 13. 9 ; 14. 3.

[*naonō*] v. l. N. 67.

naomahe ZPGl. 1. 9.

nata cf. *fra°*.

nadatum N. 46.

naðās[*ča* N. 95.

naðō Phl. Vd. 8. 74.

nafəðrō N. 47, 48 ; Vij. p. 165 ; W. 7. 1.

nafō cf. *hāmō°*.

nabā-nazdištəm N. 9.

nabā-nazdištō N. 13.

nana N. 13.

nanətəma N. 86.

namra-vāxš ZPGl. 8. 7.

nara N. 64 ; Vij. p. 139, 158, 160 ; Yt. (APZ.) 23. 1 ; ZPGl. 4. 8 ; 14. 6.

naratō N. 46, 97.

naras[*ča* N. 98 ; Yt. (Vtp.) 24. 30.

narəm N. 92 ; Phl. Vd. 3. 14 ; T. 38, 107 ; Vth. 2, 11, 13 ; Yt. (Vtp.) 24. 15, 44.

narəm[*ča* Yt. 22. 13 ; Yt. (Vtp.) 24. 59.

narəš Yt. (Vtp.) 24. 52.

narō A. 84 ; N. 28, 46 ; Phl. Vd. 8. 22 ; 15. 10 ; SkN. p. 480 ; Vij. p. 24, 25, 127, 145, 148 (2), 157 ; Yt. 22. 14 ; Yt. (Vtp.) 24. 12, 42, 60 ; ZPGl. 4. 8 ; 38. 7.

narōiṭ cf. *paiti°*.

narąm N. 20, 52 ; Phl. Vd. 5. 9 ; Vij. p. 23, 39 ; Vth. 19 ; Yt. (APZ.) 23. 1 ; Yt. (Vtp.) 24. 1, 6, 14 (3).

narąm[*ča* N. 70.

narš Pars. p. 535 ; Phl. Vd. 3. 15, 40 (2) ; T. 71, 84 ; Yt. 22. 7, 8, 10, 15 (4), 25, 26, 27–33, 37 ; Yt. (Vtp.) 24. 55, 57, 61 (3) ; ZPGl. 4. 7 ; 7. 4 ; 12. 8.

narš[*ča* T. 89.

nava Phl. Vd. 4. 10 ; 9. 32 ; 19. 21 ; T. 8.

navāzō Yt. (APZ.) **23**. 4 ; Yt. (Vtp.) **24**. 2.

naviwyåṇhamašnī Vij. p. 186 (read *aiwy°*).

nasištạm HtN. p. 484.

n(a)su Vij. p. 89.

nasukašanạm Vij. p. 89.

nasuš T. 38.

nasyehe cf. *apa°*.

našəm[ča Yt. (Vtp.) **24**. 29.

nazdišta T. 71; Yt. (Vtp.) **24**. 18.

nazdištāṯ Phl. Vd. **19**. 41.

nazdištō N. 27.

nazdyō T. 58.

nahīm cf. *x^vāθrō°*.

nā Ep. M. **1**. 4. 3 ; N. 4, 11, 17, 18, 22, 27, 30, 37, 40, 46, 65, 66, 67, 106, 108 (2); Phl. Vd. **4**. 1 ; Phl. Ys. **9**. 25 ; SlS. **8**. 22 ; T. 33, 35, 39 (in *haonā*), 123 ; Vij. p. 126, 136 ; W. Yt. **21**. 7, 9, 11, 13, 15 ; Yt. (Vtp.) **24**. 28 ; ZPGl. **4**. 1; **12**. 5. Cf. *kəm°*.

nāiri ZPGl. **12**. 5.

nāirika N. 5 (2), 6 (2), 11, 40 ; Vij. p. 24, 145, 179 (3); Vth. 3, 8, 17; ZPGl. **4**. 9.

nāirikanạm ZPGl. **4**. 9.

nāirikayāi Yt. **22**. 18; Yt. (Vtp.) **24**. 64 (2).

nāirikayå N. 59; Vij. p. 89; ZPGl. **4**. 9.

nāirikāi N. 5.

nāirikås[čiṯ N. 40.

nāirikạm N. 105 ; Yt. (APZ.) **23**. 1 ; Yt. (Vtp.) **24**. 1.

nāiribyas[ča W. **1**. 1.

nāirinạm Vij. p. 23.

nāirinạm[ča N. 70.

nairīm cf. *vasō-jạn°*.

nāiryas[ča Yt. (Vtp.) **24**. 30.

nāiryå N. 54.

nā[ča T. 23 ; Yt. (Vtp.) **24**. 28, 30.

nāfīm N. 11 ; Yt. (Vtp.) **24**. 37.

nāfō ZPGl. **10**. 7. Cf. *hạmō°*.

nānitima N. 90.

[nānō] v. l. N. 72.

nāmanō cf. *aoxtō°*.

[nāyeiatīm] v. l. T. 68.

nāyeintim T. 68.

nāvayāi N. 67.

nāhạm Phl. Vd. **3**. 29. Avestan?

niuruzdō N. 17.

nikainti Phl. Vd. **3**. 40.

niγmatəm T. 33.

nijasāiti Vij. p. 179.

nitaošayeiti N. 87.

nitəma N. 106.

nitəmaēibya N. 108.

nitəmanạm[ča Yt. (Vtp.) **24**. 23.

nitəmanạm[čiṯ Yt. (Vtp.) **24**. 23.

nitəməm N. 31 ; T. 60.

nitəm[čiṯ ZPGl. **12**. 7.

nidaδaṯ Vij. p. 97. ·

nidaδāiti Vij. p. 24.

nidaδāṯ Yt. **22**. 15 (3), 27, 33 ; Yt. (Vtp.) **24**. 61 (3).

nidāiti[ča N. 67.

nidārō Yt. (Vtp.) 24. 30.

nipātayāi Yt. (Vtp.) 24. 43.

nipāθrīm Yt. (Vtp.) 24. 14.

niwyeiti T. 32.

nimraomnō Yt. 22. 2 ; Yt. (Vtp.) 24. 54.

nimruye Yt. (Vtp.) 24. 39.

niyą A. 60.

nirāzayanti Yt. (Vtp.) 24. 36.

nivaēδaēymi N. 103.

nivaēδayemi Phl. Vd. 21. 18 (Sp.).

nivaxta[*ča* Yt. (Vtp.) 24. 38.

nivanti N. 94.

nivāitiš N. 84.

nivāitīm cf. *haθrā°*.

nisirinuyāṯ N. 52.

nistəma N. 87 (v. l. *nitəma* D.).

nisritaṯ N. 11 (2).

nisritəm N. 10.

nisrinuyāt Vij. p. 24.

nišaṇharəθrīm Yt. (Vtp.) 24. 14.

nišasti Phl. Vd. 3. 14 (v. l. *°ta*).

nišāδayōiš Yt. 22. 14.

nišhāδayōiš Yt. (Vtp.) 24. 60.

nišhiδaiti Yt. 22. 2 ; Yt. (Vtp.) 24. 54.

nišhiδōiš Yt. 22. 13 ; Yt. (Vtp.) 24. 59.

niš-hiš N. 100.

nizarəšaite Phl. Vd. 19. 30.

nizəntəm ZPGl. 40. 10.

nizdas[*ča* Vij. p. 24.

nizbaya Vij. p. 181.

nizbayaiša Yt. (Vtp.) 24. 24 (2).

nizb(*a*)*yehe* Vij. p. 139.

nižbarəmnō W. Yt. 21. 7, 9, 11, 13, 15.

nī Phl. Vd. 2. 32 (v. l.) ; Vij. p. 145 ; Yt. (Vtp.) 24. 33 (3).

nuxturušu N. 68. Cf. *ux°*.

nunč N. 11.

nū N. 46 ; Phl. Vd. 2. 32 ; T. 94, 99.

nətəma N. 27.

nətəməm ZPGl. 43. 4.

nəmaiti Yt. (Vtp.) 24. 51.

nəmaṇuhaiti Vij. p. 158.

nəmaṇhā N. 23.

nəmaṇhənti Vij. p. 160.

nəmaṇhō T. 49.

nəmas[*ča* Vij. p. 156.

nəmas[*čā* Phl. Vd. 9. 12 (2), 32 ; Vij. p. 159.

nəmasṯe Vij. p. 79 (read *nəmas tē*).

nəmaxᵛaētīš T. 75.

nəmānāi Yt. (Vtp.) 24. 33.

nəmāne Yt. (Vtp.) 24. 28, 39.

nəme Yt. 22. 20 (2) (v. l. *nəmōi* Haug); Yt. (Vtp.) 24. 65 (2).

nəmō N. 12, 28, 31, 46, 103 (2) ; Phl. Vd. 19. 18, 25 (3) ; Vij. p. 57 (2), 116 ; Yt. (Vtp.) 24. 22.

nərə N. 20.

nərəgā N. 19.

nəraṯ Phl. Vd. 3. 42.

nərə-bərəzanąm Vij. p. 146.

nərəbyas[ča W. 1. 1.
nərəbyō Phl. Vd. 4. 10 ; T. 109.
nə̄ ZPGl. 4. 1.
nō N. 20, 28, 46 (2) ; Vij. p.
133 ; Yt. (Vtp.) 24. 8, 30 ;
ZPGl. 4. 1.
nōiṱ A. 59 (4), 60 (2) ; Dk.
(P.Sj.), 3. 131 ; FD. 3 (3), 7
(3) ; N. 2, 4, 5, 6, 10 (3), 11
(2), 13, 14 (2), 15 (2), 16 (2),
17, 18, 19, 21 (2), 24 (2), 26
(2), 28, 29, 30, 38, 39, 40,
48, 52, 54 (2), 55, 56 (2), 57
(4), 58 (2), 59 (2), 60, 62, 63
(2), 65 (2), 67 (2), 68, 69 (4),
71, 85 (2), 88, 95 (2), 96 (2),
97, 98, 99, 100, 101, 104 (2),
105, 107 (3), 108, 109 (4) ;
Phl. Vd. 1. 1, 15 ; 3. 14, 40,
42 ; 8. 74 ; T. 9 (6), 12 (2),
18, 19, 23, 26 (3), 39, 66,
92 (4), 95 (4), 96, 97 (2),
99 (4), 100 (2), 102, 103 (2),
104, 105 (2), 106, 107, 117,
118, 119, 121 ; Vij. p. 25,
89 (4), 179 (2), 184 ; Vth.
10, 14, 18 ; W. 3. 1 ; 8. 11 ;
Yt. (Vtp.) 24. 28, 31 (3), 47,
51 ; ZPGl. 13. 9.
nå T. 75.
nåṇha ZPGl. 8. 1.

nåṇhaya Yt. 22. 8 (2), 26.
nåṇhābya Yt. 22. 26.
nåṇhubya Yt. (Vtp.) 24. 55 (2).
nq̨ma Vij. p. 5, 12, 50, 145
(2) ; Yt. 22. 37.
nq̨mi Bd. 14. 26 (v. l. *nq̨m*).
Probably not Avestan.
nq̨zå N. 66.
ntas[čiṱ N. 109 (read *maγnən-tas[čiṱ* cf. T. 11).
nmāṱ N. 8 (read *nmānāṱ*).
nmāna cf. *garō°*.
nmānayāiš[ča N. 95.
nmānahe N. 1, 55, 78 ; Yt.
(Vtp.) 24. 16, 17.
nmānāi N. 95.
nmanāṱ CB. (2).
nmānəm N. 8 ; Yt. (Vtp.) 24.
9.
nmāne CB. (3) ; N. 8, 61 ; T.
22.
nmānō-paiti N. 6.
nmānō-paitiš N. 5 (3).
nmānō-patōiš Yt. (Vtp.) 24. 16.
nmānō-paθni ZPGl. 5. 2.
nmānō-paθnyå Yt. (Vtp.) 24.
17.
nmānō-baxtəm T. 95.
nyāsāite W. 8. 2.
nyete T. 123 (emended from
ādarəyeitenyete).

m.

maiti N. 41 ; T. 46.
maite ZPGl. 19. 6.
maiθan Phl. Vd. 2. 28, 36 (v. l.
maθ°) Avestan ?

maiδīm Phl. Vd. 1. 3.
maiδyanq̨m N. 29.
maiδyāi N. 47 (2), 49, 50, 51 ;
Vij. p. 160.

maiδyāirya AG. 9.

maiδyāṯ N. 50.

maiδyānəm Vij. p. 181.

maiδyāyāi N. 46.

maiδyehe Vij. p. 139.

maiδyōi-paitištānō N. 86.

maiδyōi-zarəmaya AG. 5 (2).

mainaiti N. 25.

mainyava Phl. Vd. 2. 19.   Cf. *duš°*.

mainyava[*ča* W. 1. 2.

mainyavanąm Vij. p. 181.

mainyavō Yt. (Vtp.) 24. 37.

mainyutāštəm Vij. p. 181.

mainyuš A. 28 ; N. 102 ; Phl. Vd. 18. 2 ; W. 4. 2, 3 ; Yt. 22. 35 ; Yt. (Vtp.) 24. 43 47. Cf. *duš°*.

mainyū N. 34, 47 ; Phl. Ys. 46 ·end, 47 end, 48 end, 49 end; W. Yt. 21. 1 ; Yt. 22. 1.

mainyūm[*ča* N. 50 (Haug in ZPGl. 78. 9, reads °*yū*[*ča*).

mainyə̄uš HtN. p. 484 ; N. 102 (2) ; Pars. p. 534, 535 ; T. 37 ; Yt. (Vtp.) 24. 51.

maire Yt. 22. 42.

mairy- Cf. *ava°*.

mairyeiti Vth. 11.

maēainti Phl. Ys. 38. 7 (Sp.).

maēθananąm[*ča* Vij. p. 33.

maēθanəm SlS. 13. 8 (3).

maēθəmnahe Phl. Vd. 4. 1.

maēsma ZPGl. 11. 1.

maēsmana Yt. (Vtp.) 24. 31.

maēsmą T. 7.

maēšanąm N. 42, 52, 60.

maēši A. 19 ; Yt. (Vtp.) 24. 27.

maēšinəm A. 82.

maēšinąm[*ča* N. 67.

maxši Phl. Vd. 3. 14 ; ZPGl. 25. 7.

maxšyā̊ Phl. Vd. 8. 22.

maɣa ZPGl. 25. 4.

maɣanąm N. 95.

maɣəm ZPGl. 25. 7.

maɣna ZPGl. 25. 7.

maɣnəntas[*čiṯ* T. 11.

maɣnō N. 2.

maɣnąm N. 95.

maɣra Phl. Vd. 2. 40.

mata T. 46. Cf. *duš°*.

matim. Cf. *vī°*.

matrə̄š Phl. Ys. 38. 13 (Sp.).

maδaite N. 30.

maδaxahe[*ča* Phl. Vd. 1. 14.

maδi-mastəmahe T. 65.

maδimāi N. 70.

maδimya N. 33.

maδu ZPGl. 25. 6.

maδəmāi N. 70.

maδəmāṯ N. 78.

maδəməm[*ča* Vij. p. 128.

maδəmya N. 78.

maδəmyā N. 20.

maδō N. 30 (2).

maδmya N. 26.

maδmyehe ZPGl. 12. 8.

maṯ N. 47 (3), 65, 70 ; Vij. p. 139 ; ZPGl. 25. 1.

maṯ-fšum W. Yt. 21. 14.

maṯ-raθwəm W. Yt. 21. 14.

man- cf. *upa°*.

mana N. 33 ; T. 92.

manaoθra Vij. p. 125.

manaoθri ZPGl. 10. 2.

mana[*ča* T. 88.

manaṇha A. 25 ; N. 67 ; Phl. Vd. **18**. 2.

manaṇhaṭ Yt. **22**. 40.

manaṇhas[*ča* T. 57.

manaṇhā N. 47.

manaṇhe HtN. p. 485 ; Phl. Vd. **3**. 42.

manaṇhō N. 67 ; T. 31 ; W. **1**. 1. Cf. *duš°* and *hu°*.

manaṇhå T. 1.

manahe T. 80.

manahi T. 81.

manahīm T. 90, 91 ; Yt. **22**. 16, 34 ; Yt. (Vtp.) **24**. 62.

manahyehɛ[*ča* Yt. (Vtp.) **24**. 32.

maništiš Yt. (Vtp.) **24**. 37.

manō N. 22 ; T. 55, 62, 78 ; Vij. p. 128 ; W. Yt. **21**. 3 ; Yt. (Vtp.) **24**. 51. Cf. *ašto°*, *vohū°* and *hu°*.

manå A. 3. Cf. *snaoδō°* and *šātō°*.

mantā ZPGl. 17. 2.

manya A. 25.

manyaoṭ Yt. **22**. 40.

manyå T. 29.

mamanås[*ča* T. 58.

mamδya N. 26 (read *maδmya*).

mamne T. 26, 46.

mayaṭ ZPGl. 19. 6.

mayazdahe N. 81.

mayazdəm N. 28.

mayå T. 106 ; ZPGl. 25. 3.

maraotū Vij. p. 162.

maraoṭ Vij. p. 152.

marata ZPGl. 15. 1. Cf. *gayehe°*.

marahe T. 9.

marātanąm N. 58.

marəkaē[*ča* T. 6.

marəja Phl. Vd. **18**. 70.

marətanąm[*čā* N. 22 (2).

marəθrāi Yt. **22**. 38.

marənti. Cf. *afra°* and *fra°*.

marəntəm T. 15.

marəzanō. Cf. *ātarə°*.

marəždikāi A. 49 ; Dk. (P. Sj. 3. 156.

marąm Phl. Vd. **3**. 42.

marzukā Bd. **14**. 26.

mas ZPGl. 25. 2.

*masana[*ča* (to be read in T. 94 for *anamasna*[*ča*).

masana[*ča* W. Yt. **21**. 6, 8, 10, 12, 14, 16 ; Yt. **22**. 11.

masas[*ča* Yt. **22**. 12 ; Yt. (Vtp.) **24**. 58.

masānå Yt. (Vtp.) **24**. 8.

masītā Phl. Ys. **27** end.

masō N. 66, 67 ; ZPGl. 10. 4. Cf. *gairi°*.

maså ZPGl. 39. 7. Cf. *sraoni°*.

masąnå Yt. (Vtp.) **24**. 7.

mastəm N. 2.

mastəmahe T. 65. Cf. *maδi°*.

mastraγnaya ZPGl. 7. 3.

mastraγnąm ZPGl. 7. 6.

mastraɣnya ZPGl. 7. 2.

mastravanąm ZPGl. 7. 6.

masyaṇhō ZPGl. 6. 12.

masyō N. 70, 87.

maš Phl. Vd. 1. 1.

mašyāka FD. 3 ; Phl. Vd. 2. 32 ; T. 37 ; Vth. 18.

mašyākaēibyō Phl. Vd. 2. 5.

māšyākåṇhō A. 41 ; Yt. 22. 42.

mašyānahe Yt. (Vtp.) 24. 4.

mašyānąm A. 58 ; HtN. p. 484 ; Vij. p. 53 ; Yt. (APZ.) 23. 4 ; Yt. (Vtp.) 24. 6.

mašyō A. 80 ; Vij. p. 29, 89 ; ZPGl. 9. 5 ; 25. 4.

mazaṇhəm N. 45.

mazaṇhō cf. *virō°*.

mazišta Yt. (Vtp.) 24. 46.

mazišta [*ča* N. 84.

mazištahe Vij. p. 79.

mazištəm N. 61 ; Pars. p. 534 ; W. 4. 1.

mazištya Dk. (P. Sj.) 3. 131.

mazō cf. *tanu°*.

mazgəm [*ča* ZPGl. 11. 6.

mazda N. 46 ; T. 69 ; Vij. p. 99 ; W. Yt. 21. 1 ; Yt. 22. 1, 20 ; Yt. (Vtp.) 24. 20, 24, 38, 65.

mazdaðāta Vij. p. 89 ; W. Yt. 21. 3.

mazdaðātanąm N. 48 ; Vij. p. 165 ; W. 7. 1.

mazdaðātayå N. 48 ; Vij. p. 165 ; W. 7. 1.

mazdaðātahe N. 47 (2), 65 ; Phl. Vd. 19. 18 ; W. 5. 1, 2 (2).

mazdaðātāi N. 46.

mazdaðātəm N. 47.

mazdaðāte Yt. (Vtp.) 24. 22, 36.

mazdaðātō Vij. p. 136 ; Yt. (Vtp.) 24. 24.

mazdayasna N. 61, 71, 85, 103 ; Phl. Vd. 5. 7 ; Vij. p. 179, 180.

mazdayasnaēibyō Yt. (Vtp.) 24. 45.

mazdayasnīm Vij. p. 126.

mazdayasnanąm CB.; N. 11 (2), 61, 63 ; Vij. p. 145.

mazdayasnō N. 20 (2), 46 (2), 58, 103 (2) ; Vij. p. 145, 148, 160 ; W. 8. 1 ; ZPGl. 25. 4.

mazdayasnōiṯ N. 41 (2), v. l. 72.

mazdā Phl. Vd. 11. 16, 18, 20 ; Phl. Ys. 27 end ; Vij. p. 68.

mazdāi N. 46 (3) ; Phl. Vd. 19. 25 ; SlS. 13. 9 ; Vij. p. 181 ; Yt. (Vtp.) 24. 33 (2), 51 ; ZPGl. 32. 6.

mazdišta N. 60.

mazdōiš N. 72.

mazdō Vij. p. 181 read (°*då*).

mazdå A. 57 ; CB.; N. 28, 31 (5), 36, 37 (2), 46 (5), 47 (5), 49 (2), 58, 61 (3), 65 ; Pars. p. 521, 532, 535 ; Phl. Vd. 2. 32 ; Phl. Ys. 27 end ; SkN. p. 480 ; SlS. 13. 8 ; T.

1, 23, 28, 29, 32, 55, 58, 82,
88 (2), 92 ; Vij. p. 12, 50
(3), 51 (2), 52, 54, 79 (2),
99, 126, 138, 141, 152, 153,
159, 162, 164 (2); Vth. 1,
6, 14 ; W. 4. 2 ; 5. 1 ; 9. 1
(3); W. Yt. 21. 2, 7, 9, 11,
13, 15, 17 ; Yt. 22. 2 (2), 4,
6, 13, 17, 20, 38 (3), 40 ;
Yt. (APZ.) 23. 2 ; Yt. (Vtp.)
24. 11, 20, 21, 24, 33, 39,
40, 53, 54, 63 ; ZPGl. 13. 3 ;
16. 11 ; 38. 6.
mazdąm N. 61, 65, 70, 103 ;
Pars. p. 531, 534 ; Phl. Ys.
9. 27 ; T. 22 ; Vij. p. 52
(2), 54, 128 (2) ; W. 5. 2 ;
W. Yt. 21. 1, 3 ; Yt. 22. 1,
14 ; Yt. (Vtp.) 24. 14, 60.
mazdyas[*čiṯ* Yt. (Vtp.) 24. 30.
mahī Yt. (APZ.) 23. 8.
mahe W. 2. 2.
mahmāi N. 70.
mahrka- cf. *a°* and *pōuru°*.
mahrkaθəm A. 48 v. l. (Geiger)
°kasəm.
mahrkūšō W. 8. 2.
mā A. 28 ; HtN. p. 483 (4) ;
Phl. Vd. 1. 1 (*mārava?*) ; 5.
34 ; T. 4, 22 (4), 35 ; Yt. 22.
17, 35 ; Yt. (Vtp.) 24. 12 (2),
35, 37, 50, 63 ; ZPGl. 19. 6.
māaṯ ZPGl. 3. 2. *maṯ* (R.).
māi ZPGl. 19. 8.
māianuhe ZPGl. 19. 8 (r. *anuhe*).
mā[*ča* T. 90.

mā-čīm CB.
māta ZPGl. 5. 5 ; 19. 9.
mātarō N. 69 ; Phl. Ys. 38. 15
(Sp.).
mātrąm Yt. (Vtp.) 24. 50.
[*māṯ*] v. l. N. 69.
māmərənčainīš Phl. Vd. 8. 72 ;
9. 27.
māyavaitibyas[*ča* Yt. 22. 16,
34 ; Yt. (Vtp.) 24. 62.
mārava Phl. Vd. 1. 1. Cf.
mā rava.
mārənte cf. *paitiš°*.
māvaya Yt. (Vtp.) 24. 33 (2).
māzainyanąm Pars. p. 534.
māzdayasniš Yt. (Vtp.) 24. 35,
52.
māzdayasnīm Yt. (Vtp.) 24. 14.
māzdayasnōiš SlS. 13. 1 ; T.
20; Vth. 2, 7 ; Yt. (Vtp.)
24. 10, 34, 37, 42.
māhya N. 47.
māhyanąm[*ča* N. 47 ; Vij. p.
179.
miθō T. 26 (2).
miθōsāsṯ ZPGl. 35. 1. Pāzand?
miθōhitahe T. 7.
miθwa ZPGl. 25. 1.
miθnāiti cf. *ā°*.
miθra Vij. 51, 126, 127.
miθrahe N. 31 (2).
miθrəm Yt. (APZ.) 23. 6 ; Yt.
(Vtp.) 24. 4.
miθrō Phl. Ys. 10. 1, 3 ; Yt.
(Vtp.) 24. 52.
mimarō ZPGl. 25. 3.

mištəm cf. bavarə°.

mišvanahe Pars. p. 522.

miždahe Yt. (Vtp.) 24. 30.

mīry- cf. ava°.

mīždəm W. 9. 1.

muθrəm ZPGl. 25. 6.

murā ZPGl. 25. 5.

mustəməšō ZPGl. 25. 2.

mušta-masō ZPGl. 10. 3.

mūxti T. 46 (read uxti).

məθrəm N. 17.

mərəxš ZPGl. 25. 8.

mərəγa Phl. Vd. 17. 9, 11 (Sp.)

mərəγō Yt. 22. 41 (2).

mərətō W. 8. 2.   Cf. ava°.

mərənčō cf. ašəm°.

mərənčyāi[ča Phl. Vd. 1. 14.

mərəzaiti cf. fra°.

mərəzānāi ZPGl. 25. 5.

mərəzu ZPGl. 25. 1.

mərəzu-jītayō Yt. 22. 42.

mərəzu-jītīm Yt. (Vtp.) 24. 26.

mərəzu-jvəṅhō Yt. 22. 42.

mərəzvī W. 8. 2.

mərəždāta Yt. (Vtp.) 24. 31.

meždəm ZPGl. 25. 6.

mē N. 9, 46 (2), 63, 67 (v. l. mī), 68, 102 (2); T. 23, 36, 87; Vij. p. 99, 181; Yt. 22. 11; Yt. (APZ.) 23. 1; Yt. (Vtp.) 24. 1, 31 (2); ZPGl. 14. 4.

mošu ZPGl. 25. 1.   Cf. mō°.

mošu[ča W. 8. 1.

mōi N. 36, 46, 102 (3); Phl. Vd. 11. 20; 19. 10; Phl. Ys. 27 end; T. 70.

mōšu Phl. Vd. 2. 5. Cf. mo°.

må Ep. M. 1. 4. 3; ZPGl. 19. 7.

måṅha Dk. 8. 44. 27; Phl. Vd. 1. 3; 2. 41; 9. 32. Cf. xšvaš°.

måṅhahe N. 47.

måṅhəm Yt. (APZ.) 23. 6; Yt. (Vtp.) 24. 4.

måṅhəm[ča Yt. (Vtp.) 24. 43.

måṅhō Vij. p. 179, 184; W. 8. 1. Cf. xšvaš°.

maθwəm Phl. Vd. 2. 5.

maθra VS. Extr. 4. Cf. tanu° frašōšō° and haδa°.

maθrahe VS. Extr. 3; Yt. 22. 38 (3).

maθrāi VS. Extr. 1.

maθrāṭ T. 102.

maθrəm T. 3; VS. Extr. 2.

maθrō N. 2; W. 9. 1; Yt. (Vtp.) 24. 49.

maθrąs[čā T. 4.

mąnayāṯ Dk. (P. Sj.) 3. 131.

mąn(a)yən Phl. Vd. 2. 32; T. 33; Vij. p. 181.

mąm A. 25, 26, 27, 28; T. 22, 35, 37; W. Yt. 21. 3; Yt. 22, 12, 14 (2); Yt. (Vtp.) 24. 50 (2), 60 (2); ZPGl. 19. 6; 25. 3.

myaēši ZPGl. 25. 6.

myazdaē[*ča* N. 81.

myazdanąm N. 63.

myazdavanąm N. 62, 63.

myazdəm N. 28 (2); Phl. Ys. 3. 21.

myazde N. 61, 62, 81.

myazdōiš N. 83.

myō N. 37.

mraotū N. 60; Pars. p. 521; Vij. p. 164; W. 2. 1.

mraodəs[*ča* N. 53.

mraoṭ A. 57, 81; Yt. 22. 2, 4, 6, 17, 20; Yt. (Vtp.) 24. 11, 22; ZPGl. 9. 7.

mraomi W. 4. 1. Cf. *fra*°.

mraomnō cf. *ni*°.

mraxsąm cf. *a*°.

mravaṭ ZPGl. 9. 7.

mrāta cf. *amarātanąm*.

mru ZPGl. 9. 8.

mruā[*ča* N. 62.

mruta ZPGl. 25. 5.

mruye cf. *ā*° and *ni*°.

mruyå W. 1. 1. Cf. *paiti*° and *fra*°.

mrūiti N. 71.

mrūiði A. 26; Phl. Vd. 2. 5; W. 1. 2.

y.

yaēibyō Vij. p. 89.

yaē[*ča* W. 1. 2.

yaētatarə ZPGl. 16. 10.

yaētuš ZPGl. 16. 6.

yaētušāṭa ZPGl. 40. 9.

yaēva[*ča* Vij. p. 128 (read *yavaē*[*ča*).

yaēšənta ZPGl. 16. 4.

yaēšąm N. 60, 70.

yaēzō N. 37.

yaoxtavatąm Vij. p. 53.

yaoxštyō cf. *hazaṇra*°.

yaona N. 52.

yaoščini ZPGl. 16. 7.

yaoždaθaṭ N. 73, 74.

yaoždaθāiti Vij. p. 89.

yaoždaθāni Yt. (Vtp.) 24. 49.

yaoždāiti Vij. p. 179, 180. Cf. *pairi*°.

yaoždātanąm Vij. p. 138.

yaoždāθranąm Vij. p. 181.

yaoždāθryāṭ Phl. Vd. 19. 41.

yaoždāθryō Ep. M. 1. 4. 3; NkN. p. 474; Vij. p. 89, 126, 136.

yaxštis cf. *θri*°.

yaxštis[*ča* ZPGl. 16. 8.

yatō Phl. Vd. 3. 15 (D.).

yaθa A. 17 (3), 19, 82, 111; AG. 10; N. 8 (2), 9, 11, 12, 17, 22, 42, 43, 47 (2), 48, 58 (3), 65, 66 (3), 67 (2), 68 (2), 69, 70, 86, 89, 99, 103, 106, 107; Phl. Vd. 1. 14; 2. 32 (2); 3. 14; 7. 52; 8. 22 (2); 15. 10; T. 23, 33, 37, 38, 59 (2), 60, 68; Vij. p. 67, 126 (2), 128, 137, 138 (2), 181; Vth. 12; W. 1. 2; 2. 3; 6. 1 (3); 7. 1; Yt. 22. 2, 9, 11, 12, 20; Yt. (APZ) 23. 2 (8), 3 (5), 4 (5), 5 (4),

6 (5), 7 (4), 8 (2); Yt. (Vtp.)
24. 2 (5), 3 (3), 4 (5), 9 (2),
10, 12 (2), 13 (2), 20, 25, 27,
29, 33 (3), 34, 37, 46, 52,
56, 58, 59; ZPGl. 9. 6 ; 12.
7, 8, 9 ; 41. 6.
yaθa[ča Vij. p. 158; ZPGl.
13. 5.
yaθana Yt. (Vtp.) **24.** 30.
yaθā FD. 3 ; N. 2, 34, 37 (4),
46 (4); Phl. Vd. **9.** 27 ; T.
27 ; W. **9.** 1 ; ZPGl. 12. 5.
yaθā ahū vairyō Bd. **1.** 21 ; Dk.
7. 4. 41 ; Māh Yt. o ; N. 46
(4), 65 ; Pars. p. 5.21, 531,
532 ; Phl. Vd. **19.** 2, 22 ; Phl.
Ys. 28 end, 29 end, 30 end, 31
end, **32** end, **33** end, **34** end,
41. 17, **43** end, **50** end, **58.**
12, **59** end, **60** end, **62** end,
67. 41, **70** end; Pl. (8); SlS.
12. 32 ; Vij. p. 67, 98, 151
(2), 154 (2), 155, 164 ; W.
7. 1.
yaθå W. **9.** 1 (read *yaθā*).
yaθra N. 10 (4); ZPGl. 13. 3.
yaθrā N. 36 ; ZPGl. 12. 11 ;
13. 2.
yaδōiṯ N. 44, 52 (2), 83.
yaṯ A. 28, 66 ; Ep. M. **1.** 4. 3 ;
N. 4, 7, 9, 10, 19, 20, 24,
42, 43, 45, 47 (3), 48, 54 (2),
61 (4), 62 (4), 63, 65 (3), 70
(3), 73, 74, 75, 76, 81, 83,
85, 87, 103 ; Phl. Vd. **2.** 5 ;
4. 1 ; **7.** 52 ; **8.** 74 ; **15.** 10 ;

18. 43, 70 ; T. 78, 80, 81,
87, 88, 92, 93, 99, 116 ; Vij.
p. 25, 89, 126, 136 (2), 145,
146, 160, 180 ; W. **1.** 2 ; **8.**
2 (2); W. Yt. **21.** 14, 16, 17 ;
Yt. **22.** 1, 2, 11, 12, 13, 17,
19, 20, 35 ; Yt. (Vtp.) **24.** 4,
13, 20 (2), 25, 28, 33 (3),
34, 37, 42, 43, 46, 49, 51,
52, 58, 63 ; ZPGl. 11. 12.
yaṯ N. 65 (for *ūθyaṯ*).
yaṯ[čiṯ N. 42.
yantō cf. *frā°*.
yayata ZPGl. 16. 8.
yayeinti N. 97.
yayå Phl. Vd. **13.** 9.
yava N. 101 ; T. 26 ; Yt. **22.**
8, 10, 26 ; Yt. (Vtp.) **24.** 55,
57 ; ZPGl. 15. 2.
yavaē[ča Phl. Vd. **7.** 52 ; ZPGl.
17. 6.
yavaētātaē[ča FD. 7 ; ZPGl.
17. 6.
yavata ZPGl. 14. 12 ; 15. 1.
yavatahe N. 11.
yavatātaē[ča Vij. p. 128.
yavaṯ N. 12, 21 (2), 23, 38, 39,
83, 108, 109 ; Phl. Vd. **4.** 1 ;
T. 94 ; ZPGl. 14. 8 ; 41. 8.
yavaᵑhǝm A. 82.
yavanąm N. 28 (2).
yavahe ZPGl. 17. 3.
yavākǝm N. 67 ; W. **6.** 1 ;
ZPGl. 3. 9.
yave ZPGl. 11. 12.
yavō N. 69, 70, 90.

yasā N. 34.

yasō-bərətābyō Yt. 22. 38 ; ZPGl. 16. 12.

yaska cf. *ayaskəm.*

yaskā N. 62.

yas[*ča* N. 63, 82 ; Phl. Vd. 7. 52 ; T. 36 ; Yt. (Vtp.) 24. 27 (2).

yastīm cf. *darəγō°.*

yasna Vij. p. 126, 128 ; Yt. (Vtp.) 24. 20 (2), 21. Cf. *daēva°* and *mazda°.*

yasnahe N. 22 (2).

yasnāi[*ča* N. 48, 58, 61, 81 ; Pars. p. 521 ; W. 1. 2 ; Yt. (Vtp.) 24. 47 (2).

yasnəm N. 20, 22, 24, 40, 46, 65 ; T. 88.

yasnəm[*ča* N. 103 ; Pars. p. 532 ; Pl.; T. 28, 88 ; Vij. p. 97, 156 (°*nm*), 164 ; W. 2. 3 ; ZPGl. 17. 4.

yasnō Vij. p. 127.

yasnō-kərətaēibyō N. 70, 74.

yasnās[*ča* N. 48 ; W. 7. 2.

yasnᵢa N. 37.

yasnyanąm Vij. p. 148 (2).

yašta N. 46.

yaštā ZPGl. 17. 1.

yaštibyō T. 32.

yaštəm cf. *darəγō°.*

yaštā̊ W. 1. 2 (4).

yaz- cf. *fra°* and *frā°.*

yaza FD. 7 ; N. 14.

yazaēša ZPGl. 16. 12.

yazaoiščina Yt. (Vtp.) 24. 48.

yazata N. 55 ; Vij. p. 51, 54 (3), 128 (2); W. 1. 2 ; Yt. (Vtp.) 24. 7 (2).

yazatanąm N. 47, 48 ; Vij. p. 165 ; W. 5. 1 ; 7. 2 ; Yt. (APZ.) 23. 4.

yazatahe Vij. p. 79, 141.

yazatəm N. 61.

yaz[*a*]*nti* N. 61, 62.

yazamaide N. 28, 47 (9), 61, 65, 70 (2); Pars. p. 531 (3), 534 ; Phl. Vd. 2. 5 ; Vij. p. 52 (4), 156 ; W. 2. 2 ; 5. 2 (8) ; 9. 3 ; Yt. 22. 37, 38 (4).

yazāi N. 47, 70, 103 ; Yt. 22. 37 ; ZPGl. 17. 3.

yazāiti N. 22, 70 (2).

yazāne Yt. (Vtp.) 24. 20, 21.

yazi[*ča* Yt. (Vtp.) 24. 47 (read *yez°*).

yazūm Yt. (Vtp.) 24. 26.

yazəbənti N. 24.

yazənte Yt. 22. 14 ; Yt. (Vtp.) 24. 60.

yazəmna SlS. 8. 22. Cf. *a°.*

yazəmnahe N. 20.

yazəmnō Yt. 22. 13 ; Yt. (Vtp.) 24. 59.

yazōiščina Yt. (Vtp.) 24. 48.

yazdāna cf. *uz°.*

yahmaṭ A. 58 ; N. 42 ; Vij. p. 25.

yahmāi Yt. 22. 2 ; Yt. (Vtp.) 24. 53, 54.

yahmi N. 13.

yahmī N. 47.

yahmya Yt. (Vtp.) 24. 48.

yā Ep. M. 1. 4. 3 (and v. l.);
N. 4, 6, 9, 16, 22 (2), 23, 24,
37, 41, 45, 54 (3), 55 (2), 61,
62, 64, 65, 84, 94 ; Phl. Vd.
1. 14 ; 3. 15 ; 5. 49 (Av. ?);
9. 12 (2), 32 ; T. 65, 84;
Vij. p. 54, 156; W. 1. (2);
W. Yt. 21. 6, 8, 10, 12, 14,
16 ; Yt. 22. 9, 11 (2); Yt.
(Vtp.) 24. 15, 56, 58 ; ZPGl.
14. 5, 6.

yāiti N. 71.

yāirya N. 47.

yāiryanąm [*ča* N. 47.

yāiryayå N. 47.

yāiš N. 70 (2).

yākarə ZPGl. 10. 10.

[*yāgərə*] v. l. Phl. Vd. 5. 49.

yā [*ča* Yt. (Vtp.) 24. 52.

yāta N. 71.

yātayanti N. 88, 97.

yātayənte N. 88.

yātuxta ZPGl. 34. 3.

yātumatąm Vij. p. 53.

yātumastəma Phl. Vd. 1. 14.

yātumənta ZPGl. 30. 9.

yātuməntəm Phl. Vd. 1. 14.

yātəm AG. 9 ; N. 42 ; ZPGl.
15. 11.

yāθwąm ZPGl. 15. 12.

yāθra N. 108 (D. suggests
yāθrayąstuma).

yāṯ Yt. (Vtp.) 24. 43.

yānəm Yt. (Vtp.) 24. 8.

yāmə̄ng ZPGl. 14. 10.

yāraṯ N. 46 (read *fra°*?).

yārə N. 11, 42 (2), 44; ZPGl.
16. 3.

yārə-drājō Yt. (Vtp.) 24. 45.

yā [*saiti*] Phl. Vd. 7. 52.

yāsaṇha N. 103 (2).

yāsā N. 23 ; Phl. Ys. 28 end,
30 end, 31 end, 32 end, 33
end, 34 end.

yāskərəstəməm ZPGl. 16. 1.

yāsta cf. *aiwi°*.

yāzəm Yt. (Ytp.) 24. 5.

yāžəm ZPGl. 15. 7.

yāhu N. 54.

yāhya N. 3.

yijaiastiš ZPGl. 41. 8 (*yuj°* R.).

yim A. 28 (2), 77, 78, 79, 80 ;
FD. 7 ; N. 1, 61, 103 ; Pars.
p. 534 ; Phl. Vd. 7. 52 (2) ;
Phl. Ys. 9. 27 ; T. 22 ; W.
4. 1 ; W. Yt. 21. 3 ; Yt. 22.
8, 17, (2), 26, 35 (2), 38 ;
Yt. (Vtp.) 24. 10, 42 (2), 55,
63.

vimahe Phl. Vd. 2. 5.

yimō Phl. Vd. 2. 19, 32 ; Yt.
(APZ.) 23. 3.

yuxta ZPGl. 15. 8, 9.

yujayaštiš N. 8.   Cf. *yij°*.

yujiti ZPGl. 15. 8.

yum Yt. 22. 11, 12 ; Yt. (Vtp.)
24. 58.

yūnaṯ T. 67.

yūnō Yt. 22. 18, 36 ; Yt. (Vtp.)
24. 17 (2), 64.

*yūm cf. vispāyūm?

yūm[ča T. 84.

yūšmākəm W. 6. 1 ; ZPGl. 3. 9; 15. 7.

yūžəm Yt. (Vtp.) 24. 8.

yəm N. 16 ; W. 9. 2.

yō N. 35, 102; T. 112 ; Vij. p. 5 ; ZPGl. 13. 6, 7.

yeitīm cf. drājō°.

yeiti T. 64, cf. apa°, uz° and para°.

yete N. 68.

yeði ZPGl. 16. 10.

yeńhe N. 7 (2), 9, 10, 11, 46 (2), 65, 67, 102 (3); Pars. p. 532 (2); Phl. Vd. 3. 31 ; 18. 51 ; Phl. Ys. 21 end, 56. 12, 62 end, 67 end, 70 end ; T. 49.

yeń[he dā]θrahe N. 84.

yese N. 12.

yesnīm W. 1. 1.

yesne N. 67.

yesnya T. 21.

yesnyanąm N. 12 ; Yt. (Vtp.) 24. 28.

yeza[ča N. 3 (3).

yezi N. 10, 11 (2), 14, 26 (3), 27, 32, 33, 38 (2), 39 (2), 40, 42, 46, 50, 55 (4), 60, 69 (4), 88 (2), 91, 92, 94 (4), 95, 96 (2), 97, 100 (3), 101 (3), 104 (2), 105 (2), 107, 109 (2); Phl. Vd. 5. 7 ; 7. 72 ; T. 35 ; Vij. p. 23, 24 (2), 25, 145 (2), 148, 157, 179 (2); Vth. 2, 5,

7, 11, 15; Yt. (Vtp.) 24. 50.

yezii T. 12.

yeziətva N. 24.

yezi[ča N. 3 (3), 5, 80 ; Vij. p. 24.

yezəntəm N. 65.

yehyā ZPGl. 14. 7.

yēšte Vij. p. 141.

yoištō ZPGl. 15. 4.

yoxštayō ZPGl. 16. 7.

yoγəða ZPGl. 15. 4.

yoždanahe ZPGl. 16. 9.

yō A. 77, 78, 79, 80, 81 (2); Ep. M. 1. 4. 3 ; FD. 3 ; HtN. p. 484; Māh Yt. 5 ; N. 4, 6, 7, 9, 13, 14, 15, 17, 18, 19, 24, 25, 31, 32, 37 (5), 41 (2), 42, 43, 44, 45, 46, 48, 58, 60 (3), 61 (2), 69 (2), 84 (2), 87, 89, 91, 92, 93, 95 (2), 96, 97 (2), 98, 99 (2), 100 (2), 101 (2), 103 (2), 105, 109 (2); Phl. Vd. 2. 5 ; 3. 14, 40 ; 7. 52 ; 13. 34 ; T. 3, 24, 27, 45, 58, 78, 82, 91, 92, 98, 100, 102, 104, 106, 107, 110 ; Vij. p. 52, 54, 68, 89, 126, 133, 136, 160, 179, 180, 191 ; Vth. 14 ; W. 4. 2 ; 8. 1 ; W. Yt. 21. 3 ; Yt. 22. 7, 8, 10, 15 (4), 25, 26, 27–33, 37, 41 ; Yt. (APZ.) 23. 3, 4 ; Yt. (Vtp.) 24. 10 (2), 30 (2), 31 (4), 34, 43, 55, 57, 61 (3),

63; ZPGl. 7. 1, 3, 6; 13. 8;
14. 3; 15. 7; 17. 10.
yōi N. 2, 7, 20, 29, 33, 52;
Phl. Vd. 3. 40; T. 109; Yt.
(Vtp.) 24. 12, 18 (2), 32;
ZPGl. 15. 8.
yōištō N. 1.
yōjuyastoiš N. 71.
[*yōna*] v. l. N. 52.
yå N. 31, 42, 43, 44, 45, 46,
50, 54 (5), 61, 103; T. 26,
76; Vij. p. 156; W. 9. 1;
Yt. 22. 39; Yt. (Vtp.) 24.
46, 51.
yåṇha- cf. *aiwi*°.

raiθyanąm cf. *frā*°.
raēxšaiti N. 80.
raēxšīša T. 90. Cf. *paiti*°.
raēčyāṯ Vij. p. 23. Cf. *paiti*°.
raēθwa N. 67.
ra[*ē*]*θwaiti* N. 61.
raēθwayeiti N. 11, 80.
raēθwayeinti N. 62.
raēθwiš N. 66.
raēθwiš-karahe N. 76, 79.
raēθwiš-karəm N. 82.
raēθwənti N. 61.
raēre ZPGl. 28. 8.
raēva ZPGl. 28. 8.
raēvatō N. 31, 46, 47, 58, 61;
Pars. p. 521, 532, 535 (2);
Vij. p. 141, 164 (2); W. 5. 1.
raēvatąm Vij. p. 53.
raēvatąm[*ča* Yt. (Vtp.) 24. 37.
raēvaṯ-čiθrayå Yt. (Vtp.) 24. 56.

yåṇhuyanąm Vij. p. 23.
yåṇham N. 71.
yåṇhąm[*ča* N. 46.
yåṇhąm[*čā* N. 46, 65 (2).
yås[*ča* Vij. p. 99.
yą cf. *ni*°.
yąm Pars. p. 534; T. 66; Vij.
p. 24; W. Yt. 21. 7, 9, 11,
13, 15; Yt. 22. 3, 5, 10, 21–
24 (2); Yt. (Vtp.) 24. 52,
57.
yąstuma N. 108 (D. suggests
θrayąs°).
ynā N. 15.
yvaē[*ča* FD. 7.

r.

raēvantəm Pars. p. 531; W. 5.
2.
raēvas-čiθrayå Yt. 22. 9.
raēša N. 58. Cf. *tnaiš*.
raēša[*ča* N. 9.
raēšayāṯ Yt. (Vtp.) 24. 44 (2).
raēšəm Yt. (Vtp.) 24. 44.
raēše N. 2.
raēšō Yt. (Vtp.) 24. 44 (2).
raēšąm N. 71.
raēš[*ča* Pl.; Vij. p. 112; W. 2;
Yt. (APZ.) 23. 8; Yt. (Vtp.)
24. 34, 46.
raēzaēte N. 68.
raoxšnəm Yt. (Vtp.) 24. 4.
raoɣnahe A. 16; Yt. 22. 18;
Yt. (Vtp.) 24. 64.
raočaṇhəm Yt. (APZ.) 23. 8;
Yt. (Vtp.) 24. 5; ZPGl. 28,
10.

raočaṇhąm ZPGl. 42. 11. Cf. also *fragatōiṯ*.

raočay- cf. *ā°*.

raočahe N. 68.

raočahva Yt. (Vtp.) 24. 61.

raočinavantəm Yt. (Vtp.) 23. 6.

raočō T. 92.

raočōhva Yt. 22. 15.

raočā̊ N. 47 ; Phl. Vd. 2. 40 (2) ; T. 71, 83 ; W. Yt. 21. 16.

raoθəmnahe cf. *apa°*.

raoδ- cf. *hu°*.

raoδaēšva Yt. 22. 9 ; Yt. (Vtp.) 24. 56.

raoδaṯ ZPGl. 28, 9.

raoδaṇhō N. 26.

raoδayən Phl. Vd. 5. 7.

raoδayeiti N. 42, 43.

raodayeite T. 110.

raoδənti N. 42.

raoraθa Yt. (Vtp.) 24. 8.

raxsąm Yt. (Vtp.) 24. 12.

raγąm Phl. Vd. 1. 16.

ratavō N. 80, 83, 102 ; VS. Extr. 4 (2) ; Yt. (Vtp.) 24. 18 (2).

ratīš T. 64.

ratu N. 80.

ratu-xšaθrayāi Yt. 22. 18.

ratu-θwəm Yt. (Vtp.) 24. 42.

[*ratu-piθwanąm*] v. l. N. 49.

ratu-fraitīm N. 52.

rat[*u*]-*f* [*r*] *üšō* N. 60.

ratu-fritīm N. 42, 43, 53.

ratu-fritə̄e N. 62.

ratu-friš N. 19, 20, 22, 23 (2), 24, 26, 27, 37, 38 (2), 39 (2), 40, 46, 47, 49, 50, 51, 52, 53, 54 (3), 55 (4), 56 (2), 57 (3), 58, 59 (2),86, 87, 89, 90, 96, 98, 99 (2), 101 (2), 103 (2), 104, 106, 107 (3), 108 ; T. 10. Cf. *a°*.

ratu-frišu N. 102.

ratu-frišō N. 60.

ratu-frətīš N. 47 (3).

ratu-frətīš N. 47.

ratu-frəš N. 21, 22 (2), 28, 54.

ratu-fryə̄e N. 31.

ratu-fryō N. 31, 32, 39, 52, 60, 87, 88, 91, 92, 93, 94, 95, 97.

ratubya ZPGl. 13. 12.

ratubyō N. 47.

ratumaṯ T. 13.

ratus N. 5.

ratuš N. 10, 19, 37 (2), 60, 72. 73, 83, 92, 98, 103 ; Phl. Vd, 9. 27 ; Vij. p. 152 ; Yt. (Vtp.) 24. 42.

ratūm N. 61 ; Vij. p. 184 ; W. 2. 2.

ratūm[*ča* Pars. p. 534.

ratūš Yt. (Vtp.) 24. 18.

ratō cf. *dāštō°*.

raθa Yt. (Vtp.) 24. 48.

raθaēštārahe Yt. (APZ.) 23. 5 ; Yt. (Vtp.) 24. 3, 16.

raθaēštārəm Yt. (Vtp.) 24. 26.

raθič N. 109. Avestan ?

raθəs[*ča* N. 97.

raθō N. 37.

raθwaiti N. 62.

raθwaē̆[ča N. 81 (2).

raθwayāṯ N. 76.

raθwas[ča N. 48 ; Vij. p. 166 (2) ; W. 7. 2.

raθwiškarahe Yt. (Vtp.) 24 15.

raθwəm cf. maṯ°.

raθwe N. 105.

raθwō N. 47 (5), 61 (2) ; Phl. Ys. 22. 5 ; Vij. p. 88, 157, 188 ; VS. Extr. 3, 4.

raθwąm N. 42 (2), 61, 82, 83 ; Phl. Ys. 27 end.

raθwya ZPGl. 13. 12.   Cf. a°.

raθwyasnąm W. 2. 2.

raθwā̊ ZPGl. 9. 2.

rapantąm cf. stē°.

rapayāṯ N. 26.

rapiθwanąm N. 49.

rapiθwayāṯ N. 49.

rapiθwitaraēibyō Yt. 22. 7.

rapiθwitaraṯ Yt. 22. 7.

rafnahīm cf. vouru°.

rafnə̄ ZPGl. 28. 8.

ranhąm T.68 ; Yt. (APZ.) 23. 4.

rayatō N. 23.

rayōiš N. 19.

rava Phl. Vd. 1. 1 (mārava ?).

ravas[ča N. 47.

rasō Phl. Vd. 6. 26.

rašayanti N. 80.

rašnuš Phl. Vd. 13. 9 ; Yt. (APZ.) 23. 7.

rašnuš[ča Yt. (Vtp.) 24. 52.

rašvatąm[ča Yt. (Vtp.) 24. 10.

razištō Phl. Vd. 13. 9 ; Yt. (Vtp.) 24. 52.

razō ZPGl. 28. 9.

razągąda N. 48.

razrazdāi T. 3 (read azrazdāi).

rāiti W. 9. 2.

rāitī cf. frā°.

rāuininąm N. 83.

rājim ZPGl. 28. 9.

rāta Yt. (Vtp.) 24. 36.

ratayō T. 75, 76.

rātā[ča Yt. (Vtp.) 24. 8.

rātōiš N. 69.

rātąm T. 70.

rāθa cf. naēmi°.

rāna ZPGl. 11. 3.

rāmanō N. 47 ; Yt. (APZ.) 23. 7.

rām(a)s[ča Vij. p. 127.

rāmištąm cf. aojō°.

rāmō-dāitīm Phl. Vd. 1. 2.

rāstəm ZPGl. 28. 9.

rāza N. 84.

rāzayanti cf. ni°.

rāzarə T. 69.

rāzarə[ča CB.

rāząm ZPGl. 18. 6.

ričyeihe N. 55.

ririšiā N. 95.

rus[ča N. 95.

rəitīm[ča T. 89.   Cf. ā°.

rəja cf. asma°.

V.

va Ganj. 5 (3), 6 (3); Mād-ch.
12 (3); N. 24, 94 (cf.
vaδāityō in N. 107); ZPGl.
2. 6.
vaie ZPGl. 2. 6.
vaikayō ZPGl. 22. 5.
vaite ZPGl. 23. 7. Cf. *saite*.
vaiδayeiti cf. *aiwi°*.
vaiδim ZGPl. 23. 1.
vaiδe cf. *saiδe*.
vaibya ZPGl. 2. 6.
vairīm A. 28 (MS. has *°im*);
N. 20, 34, 81 ; Pars. p. 531 ;
W. 9 (4).
vairya AG. 7 ; W. 1. 1.
vairyanąm N. 102.
vairyāṯ N. 68.
vairyehe Dk. (P. Sj.) 3. 156;
T. 54.
vairyō Bd. 1. 21 ; Māh Yt. o ;
N. 36, 37 (4), 46 (4), 65 ;
Pars. p. 531, 532 ; Phl. Vd.
9. 27 ; 19. 2 (5), 10, 22 ;
Phl. Ys. 28 end, 29 end, 30
end, 31 end, 32 end, 33, 34,
41. 17, 43 end, 50, 58. 12,
59 end, 60 end, 62 end, 67.
41, 70 end ; Pl (8); W. 2.
3 ; 6. 1 (3); 7. 1 ; 9. 1 (2);
W. Yt. 21. 4 ; Yt. (APZ.)
23. 8. Cf. also *yaθā ahū*
vairyō.
vairyą N. 50.
vaēijō ZPGl. 23. 6 (R. reads
vaiējō).

vaēibya Phl. Vd. 13. 34 (2), 85,
102 (Sp.) (2).
vaēča ZPGl. 11. 10.
vaēčạnti N. 100.
vaēθa N. 40.
vaēθaṯ N. 11, 68.
vaēδa N. 38 (2).
vaēδaēymi cf. *ni°*.
vaēδaṇhō Phl. Vd. 1. 15
(2).
vaēδayana cf. *baēvarạ°*.
vaēδayama ZPGl. 22. 11.
vaēδā ZPGl. 12. 5.
vaēnaθa N. 11.
vaēnaṯ ZPGl. 22. 12.
vaēnaya Phl. Ys. 9. 35.
vaēnāṯ N. 16.
vaēnōiṯ T. 33. Cf. *paiti°*.
vaēm Yt. (Vtp.) 24. 32 ; ZPGl.
22. 11.
vaēmanāṯ N. 72.
vaēyya N. 99.
vaēsaēte T. 122.
vaēščayeiti N. 99.
vaouru Vij. p. 126.
vaočata T. 22.
vaočatā T. 13.
vaočā Phl. Vd. 19. 10.
vaočāma cf. *fra°*.
vaočim W. 9. 2.
vaočīš cf. *afra°*.
vaonarạ N. 70.
vaoze T. 105, 106.
vaohxte ZPGl. 22. 3.
vaōčamå T. 29.

vaakrəm ZPGl. 22.ᵭ6.ʿ[*vank*°
(R.).

vakąuvarōiš ZPGl. 22. 9.

vaxāt̰ N. 51.

vaxəðrås[*ča* Yt. (Vtp.) 24. 37,
59.

vaxta cf. *ni*°.

vaxš W. 9. 1.   Cf. *xšayat̰*° and
hu°.

vaxša cf. *ātar*°, *ātra*° and *āθra*°.

vaxšaθəm W. 9. 2 ; Yt. (Vtp.)
24. 39.

vaxšaθəm[*ča* Vt. (Vtp.) 24. 49.

vaxšat̰ N. 47 ; T. 1.

vaxšaŋha ZPGl. 8. 12.

vaxšayat̰ cf. *aiwa*°.

vaxšayōit N. 81.

vaxsāt̰ cf. *hu*°.

vaxšisąm N. 97.

vaxšyā N. 50.

vaγðanahe N. 65.

vaγðanāt̰ Yt. 22. 2 ; Yt. (Vtp.)
24. 54.

vaγðanəm Vij. p. 116 ; ZPGl.
7. 4 ; 10. 1 ; 12. 8.

vaγžibiš N. 41, 67, 103.

vača N. 20 (2), 26, 33, 34 ;
Phl. Vd. 4. 1 ; Phl. Ys. 9.
25 ; W. 1. 1 ; 9. 2 ; Yt.
(Vtp.) 24. 39 ; ZPGl. 8. 5.

vačaiti T. 94.

vačaštvat̰ N. 24.

vačaŋha N. 67.

vačaŋhā N. 22.

vačaŋhō T. 49.   Cf. *uxða*°,
duž° and *h*°.

vačaŋhąm N. 46.

vačas[*ča* N. 60 ; T. 58.

vačasta N. 24.

vačastašti N. 33.

vačastaštivat̰ N. 23.

vačastaštīm N. 42.

vačastaštəm N. 50 (Haug in
ZPGl. 78. 9 reads °*tištəm*).

vačastəma cf. *arš*° and *uxðō*°.

vačahim cf. *θri*°.

vačim[*ča* N. 72.

vačō N. 22, 26, 33 ; W. 1. 1,
2 ; 9. 1 ; W. Yt. 21. 14 ; Yt.
22. 20 ; Yt. (Vtp.) 24. 20,
22, 26, 28, 53.   Cf. *hvačō*.

vačō-urvaitiš Phl. Vd. 7. 52 (2).

vačā̊ Phl. Vd. 2. 10 ; T. 29 ;
ZPGl. 8. 10 ; 9. 6, 9.   Cf.
āfrī°, *snaoðō*° and *haiθəm*°.

vačąm N. 33, 37 ; Vij. p. 24 ;
Yt. (Vtp.) 24. 39.   Cf. *uxðō*°.

vatim cf. *fra*°.

vatəm cf. *vasō*°.

vaðairayoš ZPGl. 22. 9.

vaðaγa ZPGl. 22. 12.

vaðāityō N. 107 (read *va dāityō*).

vafra ZPGl. 22. 3.

vafrō Yt. (APZ.) 23. 4 ; Yt.
(Vtp.) 24. 2.

vanuhi Phl. Vd. 19. 18 ; Yt.
(Vtp.) 24. 8, 22.

vanuhibyō W. 7. 1.

vanuhinąm Phl. Ys. 67. 56
(Sp.).

vanuhīm CB. ; Yt. (Vtp.) 24.
50.

vaṇuhīš Yt. 22. 13 ; Yt. (Vtp.) 24. 59.

vaṇuhēbyō Vij. p. 165.

vaṇuhya Vij. p. 139.

vaṇri ZPGl. 23. 7.

vaṇhaiti N. 92, 95 ; Yt. 22. 1, 3, 5, 19 ; Yt.(Vtp.)24. 53, 54.

vaṇhaṭ N. 71. Cf. *saṇhaṭ*.

vaṇhana[*ča* W. Yt. 21. 6, 8, 10, 12, 14, 16 ; Yt. 22. 11.

vaṇhanəm[*ča* Vij. p. 181.

vaṇharəštas[*čiṭ* N. 83, 109 ; T. 11.

vaṇhave Phl. Vd. 3. 42.

vaṇhavaēibyas[*ča* N. 108.

vaṇhāparəm Phl.Vd. 13. 2, 3, 4.

vaṇhānahe N. 92.

vaṇhānō ZPGl. 23. 7.

vaṇhi T. 65.

vaṇhibyō N. 48, 71.

vaṇhīnąm N. 20, 48 (Haug in ZPGl. 76. 20 reads °*huīn*°).

vaṇhīm T. 66.

vaṇhīš T. 115 ; Yt. (Vtp.) 24. 3.

vaṇhu[*ča* N. 46 (2).

vaṇhuna[*ča* T. 94.

vaṇhuya N. 52.

vaṇhuyå N. 47 (3), 61.

vaṇhuš N. 46 ; W. 7. 2.

vaṇhušō T. 56.

vaṇhənti N. 91.

vaṇhən N. 70.

vaṇhəm cf. *dātō*°.

vaṇhəuš N. 48 ; T. 114 ; Vij. p. 126.

vaṇhəuš[*ča* T. 31 (2).

vaṇhå Phl. Vd. 7. 52 (v. l. °*åṭ*); ZPGl. 9. 5.

vaṇhås]*ča* N. 46 (2).

vaṇhąm ZPGl.10. 8. Cf. *čiθra*°.

vaṇhas[*ča* N. 91 ; Yt. (Vtp.) 24. 58.

vaṇhazdå W. 1. 2.

vaṇhe Yt. (Vtp.) 24. 30, 36.

vaṇhō N. 48 ; Yt. (Vtp.) 24. 30.

van- cf. *a*°.

vana N. 9 ; T. 111 ; Vij. p. 5 ; ZPGl. 22. 4.

vanaite ZPGl. 22. 4.

vanainti N. 70, 84.

vanaintīm[*ča* W. 5. 2.

vanaintyås[*ča* W. 5. 1.

vanaēma N. 99.

vanaēmā ZPGl. 14. 7.

vanatąm Yt. (Vtp.) 24. 6. (2) ; ZPGl. 12. 4.

vanaṭ Phl. Vd. 7. 52 (2).

vananō N. 61.

vananti N. 84.

vanantō N. 47 (3).

vanarə ZPGl. 22. 6.

vanasti N. 109

vanāne Yt. (Vtp.) 24. 25.

vanəntō Vij. p. 136.

vanō Vij. p. 5.

vayaēibyas[*ča* Yt. 22. 16, 34 ; Yt. (Vtp.) 24. 62.

vayaoš A. 77, 78, 79, 80, 81 ; Yt. (Vtp.) 24. 24.

vayantanąm N. 26.

vayeō N. 8 (v. l. *vayṭō*).

vayō N. 47 ; Vij. p. 87 ; ZPGl.
2. 8 ; 43. 10.

vayōiš N. 47.

vayås[*čiṯ*ZPGl. 2. 9, 10 (°*åsə*[*čiṯ*
R.).

varaxəðrås[*ča* Yt. 22. 13.

varanava ZPGl. 22. 12.

varanō Vij. p. 181.

varaṇhana N. 54.

varaṇhəm cf. *garəmō°*.

varas[*ča* ZPGl. 13. 11.

varišta N. 29.

variščǎ̊ N. 85.

variš-staṇhas[*ča* N. 103.

varəina ZPGl. 23. 1.

varəkahe ZPGl. 22. 6.

varəčaṇuhatąm Vij. p. 53.

varəčǎ̊ ZPGl. 22. 7. Cf. *aš°*.

varətata ZPGl. 23. 5.

varəθra ZPGl. 22. 7.

varədaθəm Yt. (Vtp.) 24. 39.

varəða ZPGl. 11. 7.

varəðaya ZPGl. 22. 10.

varəðōs[*ča* N. 97.

varənaṇhąm Yt. (Vtp.) 24. 37

varənāiš cf. *duž°*.

varənō Yt. (Vtp.) 24. 50.

varənås[*ča* N. 92.

varəntayənti N. 97.

varənyanąm[*ča* Pars. p. 535.

varəm N. 3.

varəmanō ZPGl. 12. 2.

varəsa Vij. p. 83, 125 (2).

varəsanąm Vij. p. 127.

varəsəm Vij. p. 89, 128.

varəsəm[*ča* Vij. p. 126.

varəsō N. 90, 108 ; Vij. p. 126,
155.

varəš N. 18.

varəšajim cf. *hamō°*.

varəšahe N. 58.

varəš[*ča* N. 99.

varəštayō cf. *uz°*.

varəštas[*ča* N. 109.

varəštahe ZPGl. 3. 4.

varəštąm N. 46 ; W. 9. 2.

varəšnahe N. 106.

varəšnǎ̊ N. 52, 60.

varəšyō ZPGl. 22. 10.

varəza A. 27. Cf. *gavāstryā°*
and *sraošā°*.

varəzi cf. *bərəzaṯ°*.

varəzič N. 109. Avestan.

varəzyāṯ cf. *uz°*.

varə N. 6.

varō T. 117 ; ZPGl. 10. 5 ; 22.
10.

varō-jinō Yt. (Vtp.) 24. 37.

varō-žintəm Yt. 22. 13.

varō-žəntəm Yt. (Vtp.) 24.
59.

vartō ZPGl. 23. 5.

varsa ZPGl. 6. 7.

varšta cf. *duž°* and .*baoðō°*.

varštas[*čiṯ* N. 83.

varšti T. 46, 57. Cf. *araθwyō°*.

varšnahe FD. 7.

vavaxða ZPGl. 23. 6.

vavača T. 26.

vavačata ZPGl. 25. 2.

vavarəza T. 26.

vavāstrinam ZPGl. 40. 5.

vasas [*ča* N. 46 ; Phl. Ys. 51
end.

vasɔn Phl. Vd. **5.** 7.

vasə̄-xšayɑ̨s Yt. **22.** 2 ; Yt.
(Vtp.) **24.** 53.

vaso-xšaθrɑ̨m ZPGl. 11. 8.

vasō Vij. p. 89.

vasō-jɑ̨n-nāirīm Yt. (Vtp.) **24.**
23.

vasō-vatəm Yt. (Vtp.) **24.** 23.

vasta W. **9.** 2 ; Yt. (Vtp.) **24.**
26, 40.

vastarɑ̨m Vij. p. 136, 138,
139.

vastəmo T. 98.

vastra N. 93 ; Yt. (Vtp.) **24.**
45 ; ZPGl. 22. 1. Cf. *pasu°*.

vastranɑ̨m Vij. p. 23.

vastrahe N. 86, 91 (2).

vastrāṭ ZPGl. 18. 5.

vastrəm N. 48, 93 ; Vij. p. 180,
181.

vastrvi Vij. p. 138.

vasnā W. **9.** 2.

vasmi ZPGl. **22.** 1.

vašāta T. 105.

vaši N. 9.

vazanō cf. *ātarə°*.

vazəmnō N. 37 ; T. 10.

vazō N. 37 ; Phl. Vd. **6.** 26.

vahišta Phl. Ys. **59** end (Sp.) ;
T. 87 ; W. **1.** 1 ; **3.** 2 ; Yt.
(Vtp.) **24.** 37, 42.

vahišta N. 84.

vahištahe N. 49 (2) ; T. 106,
108 ; ZPGl. **14.** 1.

vahištā N. 36 ; • Phl. Ys. **27**
end.

vahištāaṭ [*ča* Yt. **22.** 40.

vahištāi N. 39, 109 ; Phl. Vd.
19. 18 ; Phl. Ys. **59** end
(Sp.); T. 72 ; Yt. (Vtp.) **24.**
33.

vahištāištiš N. 34.

vahištābyō N. 46.

vahištəm N. 39, 50, 67, 109 ;
Pars. p. 531 ; Phl. Vd. **19.** 18 ;
Phl. Ys. **20.** 1 ; T. 13, 28,
43, 113 ; W. **3.** 2 ; Yt.
(APZ.) **23.** 8 ; Yt. (Vtp.) **24.**
5, 32 ; ZPGl. **23.** 2.

vahištəm [*ča* T. 83.

vahištō T. 92, 112.

vahištōištōiš Yt. (Vtp.) **24.** 53.

vahištō-urvānō A. 3 ; Vij. p.
191.

vahištå Yt. (Vtp.) **24.** 3.

vahɔhīš N. 70 (for *vahɔ hīš*).

vahmāi ZPGl. **22.** 1.

vahmāi [*ča* N. 58, 61, 81 ;
Pars. p. 521 ; W. **1.** 2 ; Yt.
(Vtp.) **24.** 47.

vahməm Vij. p. 97.

vahməm [*ča* Pars. p. 532 ; Pl ;
T. 28, 88 ; ZPGl. **17.** 5.

vahmɑ̨s [*ča* N. 48 ; W. **7.** 2.

vahyō Dk. **8.** 46. 2.

vahyå T. 29.

vā A. 17 (3), 48, 51 ; Dk. (P.
Sj.) **3.** 131 ; N. **1** (2), 2, 3
(2), 5 (3), 6, 7, 9 (2), 10 (3),
14 (2), 15 (8), 16 (2), 17 (2),

18 (3) for first *vā* read v. l.
nā, 20 (2), 23, 24 (2), 25 (3),
26 (4), 27, 32 (3), 37 (9), 41
(2), 42 (3), 43 (2), 44 (2), 45
(3), 47, 58 (3), 61 (4), 62 (2),
64, 65 (2), 69 (4), 83 (4),
84, 95, 97, 99, 100 (3), 101
(2), 102 (6), 103 (4), 105
(3), 109 (2); Phl. Vd. **4**. 1 ;
7. 43 (2), 52 ; **8**. 22 ; T. 5
(3), 8, 10 (5), 34 (3), 59, 107
(2) ; Vij. p. 23 (2), 83 (2),
87 (2), 89 (2), 125 (2), 128
(2), 181 (2); Vth. 5 ; W.
Yt. **21**. 5 ; Yt. (Vtp.) **24**. 10
(3), 13 (3), 23 (3), 25, 28
(2), 44 (5), 49 (4); ZPGl.
12. 5 (2).

vāiti Yt. **22**. 8, 26; ZPGl.
34. 6.

vāitiša N. 90.

vāxš W. Yt. **21**. 4 ; ZPGl. **8**. 5,
8, 11. Cf. *xšayaṯ°* and
namra°.

vāxš-bərətibyō ZPGl. 9. 1.

vāča N. 15, 27.

vāčaṯ N. 32.

vāčayāði N. 24.

vāčim N. 14 (2), 42, 73, 103.

vāčim[ča N. 24.

vāčəm Vij. p. 24, 45 ; Yt. **22**
41 ; ZPGl. 22. 8.

vāčō N. 71.

vātaēibyō Yt. **22**. 7, 25 ; Yt.
(Vtp.) **24**. 55.

vātahe N. 47.

vātəm Yt. **22**. 8 (2), 26 (2) ; Yt.
(Vtp.) **24**. 55 (3); ZPGl.
22. 8.

vātō Yt. **22**. 7, 8, 25, 26 ; Yt.
(Vtp.) **24**. 24.

vāθmaini N. 15.

vānataṃ Yt. (Vtp.) **24**. 6 (2).

vāraiti ZPGl. 22. 10.

vārəθraɣnibyō ZPGl. 9. 1.

vārəθraɣnəš W. **9**. 1.

vārəmnəm AG. 8.

vāvō cf. *upa°*.

vāstārəm Dk. **8**. 48. 2 ; Phl.
Vd. **19**. 2, 10, 22 ; W. **9**. 2.

vāstranąm[ča N. 83.

vāstrayaṇhva ZPGl. 24. 1.

vāstrahe N. 31. Cf. *isaṯ°*, and
saṯ°.

vāstri Phl. Vd. **19**. 41.

vāstrəm N. 87.

vāstre Phl. Vd. **8**. 103 ; **9**. 294.

vāstryaθa Yt. (Vtp.) **24**. 11.

vāstryanta Yt. (Vtp.) **24**. 41.

vāstryāṯ N. 42, 43, 69 (2), 83,
109.

vāstryehe Yt. (APZ.) **23**. 5 ; Yt.
(Vtp.) **24**. 3, 16.

vāhe N. 7.

vāhš T. 53 (read *vāxš*).

viusaiti ZPGl. 22. 5.

vixaδaṯ Phl. Vd. **2**. 32.

vičā ZPGl. 23. 6.

vičidārō ZPGl. 23. 5.

vitasti ZPGl. 22. 2 ; 41. 1.

vitasti-drājō Phl. Vd. **5**. 4.

viduš ZPGl. 22. 2.

viðava ZPGl. 5. 3.

viðu ZPGl. 5. 3 (*va°* R.).

viðya[*ča* Yt. (Vtp.) 24. 15.

viðvå N. 60.

viptəm Phl. Vd. 7. 52.

vinaṯ cf. *aiwi°*.

vinānθaṯ N. 5.

vindaṯ ZPGl. 22. 2.

virō-mazaṇhō ZPGl. 16. 3.

viråðayeiti N. 11.

vivišdātō ZPGl. 17. 9.

vise ZPGl. 21. 11.

visō ZPGl. 21. 11.

vistaēšva N. 16.

viste ZPGl. 21. 11.

vispa[*ča* ZPGl. 13. 12.

vispāi ZPGl. 11. 13.

viš N. 5, 55.

viša-gaitayāaṯ[*ča* Yt. 22. 36.

višayāaṯ[*ča* Yt. 22. 36.

višāpahe N. 48.

vizuta ZPGl. 40. 4.

vī N. 27, 98 (3), 99, 108 ; T.ʼ 28, 35 ; Yt. (Vtp.) 24. 38, 55, 63 ; ZPGl. 4. 2.

vīidīm T. 52.

vīurvištiš Yt. 22. 35.

vīurvištīm Yt. 22. 17.

vīurvištīm Yt. (Vtp.) 24. 63.

vīkaiehe ZPGl. 43. 7.

vīkaya Ep. M. 1. 6. 6. ; 2. 2. 8.

[*vīčayå*] v. l. N. 8.

vīčarayatəm N. 79.

vīčarəntu CB.

vīčiθra N. 108.

vīčiθrəm[*čiṯ* SkN. p. 480 ; ZPGl. 38. 19.

vīčiθrə[*čiṯ* Ep. M. 1. 7. 4.

vījasāṯ Yt. (Vtp.) 24. 38.

vītayå N. 8.

vīṯāiti T. 18.

vīṯvā T. 35.

vīdaēvahe VS. Extr. 3.

vīdaēvāi VS. Extr. 1.

vīdaēvō N. 58.

vīdāyāṯ N. 68.

vīdārayəntəm Vth. 14.

vīdiðārəmnō Yt. 22. 7, 25 ; Yt. (Vtp.) 24. 55.

vīdōyūm VS. Extr. 2.

vīðāryaṯ Vij. p. 25.

vīðuš-ašəm Yt. (Vtp.) 24. 15.

vīðūšås[*ča* T. 77.

vīðōtuš cf. *astō°*.

vīpaiti[*čiṯ* N. 41.

vībaṇhəm Yt. (Vtp.) 24. 26.

vībarāṯ N. 108.

vībāzva Phl. Vd. 9. 32 ; 19. 21.

vīnaoiti N. 58.

vīnāṯ N. 5.

vīmatim N. 65.

vīmā N. 5.

vīra Dk. (P. Sj.) 3. 131.

[*vīraozayeiti*] v. l. N. 11.

vīraja A. 78.

vīraṇhāðō A. 78.

vīrəm cf. *paiti°*.

vīrōiði N. 11.

vīvaṇhanahe Phl. Vd. 2. 5.

vīvarə N. 39 (read *vīdarə*).

vīvarəi N. 39 (read *vīdarə*).

vīvarås [ča T. 36.

vīvahua N. 103.

vīvāpås [ča T. 36.

vīsaiti N. 19 ; T. 121.

vīsata T. 87.

vīsaṯ N. 8 ; Phl. Vd. 3. 14.

vīsāi FD. 6 ; N. 46. SlS. 13. 1.

vīsāiti N. 13.

vīsāδa N. 31, 61 (2).

vīsāmadaē [ča A. 1.

vīsəm N. 8 ; T. 5.

vīsəmnō cf. ə°.

vīse N. 8 ; T. 22.

vīsō Yt. (Vtp.) 24. 16.

vīstəm N. 54.

vīspa AG. 10 ; N. 80 ; Phl. Vd. 2. 40 (2) ; T. 94 ; Vij. p. 5, 54 ; W. 3. 1, 2 (12) ; W. Yt. 21. 3, 15 ; Yt. (Vtp.) 24. 46 ; ZPGl. 21. 11.

vīspaēibyo N. 11, 20, 47 (3), 65, 70.

vīspaē [ča T. 61.

vīspaēšu N. 13 (2) ; T. 56 (2).

vīspaēšąm N. 47 (2), 48 (2), 49 ; Vij. p. 127 (2) ; W. 5. 1.

vīspaēšąm [ča N. 60, 65.

vīspa [ča W. Yt. 21. 16.

vīspatōiš Yt. (Vtp.) 22. 16.

vīspanąm N. 22, 38, 39, 59, 68 ; Pars. p. 534, 535 (2) ; T. 93 ; Vij. p. 24, 133, 139, 157 ; W. 4 (2) ; W. Yt. 21. 1 (2) ; Yt. (Vtp.) 24. 50.

vīspanąm [ča N. 48 ; Vij. p. 89, 165 ; W. 3. 2 ; 7. 1.

vīspaya N. 69.

vīspayå N. 47 (2), 81 ; W. 9. 3.

vīsparaṯ Phl. Vd. 2. 32.

vīspahe N. 84 ; T. 58 ; Yt. (Vtp.) 24. 36.

vīspā T. 84 (really vīspayūm).

vīspāi FD. 6 ; N. 20 ; SlS. 13. 6.

vīspāis T. 2.

vīspaē [ča Vij. p. 89.

vīspəm N. 42 (2), 43 ; Phl. Vd. 7. 52 ; T. 43, 79 ; Vij. p. 89 ; W. Yt. 21. 14, 16 ; Yt. 22. 2, 20.

vīspəm [ča W. 5. 2.

vīspe HtN. p. 484 ; N. 39 (2), 60 ; Yt. (Vtp.) 24. 18.

vīspe-baxtəm T. 95.

vīspe-naēmąm ZPGl. 9. 13.

vīspō Yt. (Vtp.) 24. 15 (7), 16 (7), 17 (6); ZPGl. 11. 11.

vīspō-afsmanąm Yt. (Ytp.) 24. 14.

vīspō-xšapō N. 53.

vīspō-paēsō Yt. (Vtp.) 24. 33.

vīspō-paθa Yt. (Vtp.) 24. 28.

vīspōpit Phl. Ys. 38. 14 (Sp.) (for Av. vīspō-paitīš).

vīspō-vərəzyąm Yt. (Vtp.) 24. 14.

vīspō-hankərəθyąm Yt. (Vtp.) 24. 14.

vīspō-xᵛāθrəm Yt (APZ.) 23. 8 ; Yt. (Vtp.) 24. 5.

vīspā̊ N. 31 ; T. 63, 124; Vij.
p. 5 ; Yt. (Vtp.) 24. 51.
vīspā̊s[ča N. 75.
vīspąm Yt. (Vtp.) 24. 14 (3).
vīšavayeinte Phl. Vd. 2. 32.
vīšā[ča Phl. Ys. 31. 20.
vīšāpahe N. 48.
vīštaspa Yt. (Vtp.) 24. 1 (2), 6,
8, 9, 10, 12, 19, 24, 26, 28,
34, 37, 40, 43, 45, 53, 65.
vīštaspahe Yt. (APZ.) 23. 1.
vīštāspā Yt. (Vtp.) 24. 21.
vīštāspāi Yt. (APZ.) 23. 2, 5 ;
Yt. (Vtp.) 24. 13, 22, 45.
vīzuš Phl. Vd. 5. 32 (2).
vīzuš[ča N. 57.
vīzvå̄hu W. 4. 3.
vərəčainti cf. aipi°.
vərətka ZPGl. 10. 12.
vərədatəm W. 9. 2.
vərədā ZPGl. 14. 7.
vərədvō ZPGl. 22. 4 ; 23. 4.
vərəδka Phl. Vd. 18. 70.
vərəθraɣna AG. 9.
vərəθraɣnahe W. 5. 1 ; W. Yt.
21. 4.
vərəθraɣnāi Yt. (Vtp.) 24. 37.
vərəθraɣnəm W. 9. 2 ; Yt.
(APZ.) 23. 7 ; Yt. (Vtp.) 24.
39, 42.
vərəθraɣnəm[ča W. 5. 2 ; Yt.
(Vtp.) 24. 6.
vərəθraja Yt. (Vtp.) 24. 30.
vərəθrajå̄ Yt. (APZ.) 23. 2.
vərəθrająsta[ča Yt. 22. 11 ; Yt.
(Vtp.) 24. 58.

vərəθrająstəmō W. 9. 1.
vərəθrāi N. 68.
vərəθrāɣanō W. 9. 1.
vərəθrājanəm Yt. (APZ.) 23.
6.
vərəθrəm[ča Pars. p. 531.
vərənavaṯ ZPGl. 23. 3.
vərənyate ZPGl. 23. 4.
vərəsō N. 62.
vərəzantəm T. 15.
vərəzantō N. 52.
vərəzantąm N. 85.
vərəzintəm Yt. (Vtp.) 24. 52.
vərəzənti N. 60, 62.
vərəzyaṯ ZPGl. 23. 4.
vərəzyanti N. 6.
vərəzyāṯ N. 6 (3).
vərəzyeiti N. 48.
vərezyōit N. 16 ; Phl. Vd. 8.
103 ; 9. 294 ; 19. 41.
vərəzyąn T. 27.
vərəzyąm cf. vīspō°.
vəhrkayå̄ N. 59.
vəhrkavaiti A. 19 ; Yt. (Vtp.)
24. 27.
vəhrkahe ZPGl. 22. 5.
vehrkāi N. 17 ; T. 3.
vəhrkāṯ A. 19 ; Yt. (Vtp.) 24.
27.
vəhrkəm Phl. Vd. 7. 52.
vəhrkō N. 3 (2).
və̄ N. 103 ; SlS. 13. 1 ; T. 4 ;
Vij. p. 57 ; ZPGl. 4. 1.
voiō ZPGl. 39. 2.
voiθwa ZPGl. 23. 3.
vouru-dōiθra Yt. (Vtp.) 24. 8.

vouru-rafnahīm Yt. (Vtp.) 24.
14.

vostrəm ZPGl. 23. 3.

vohu FD. 7 ; N. 28, 65, 67 ;
Phl. Vd. 18. 2 ; T. 55 ; Yt.
(Vtp.) 24. 30, 51.

vohu-jīti Yt. (Vtp.) 24. 1.

vohuni ZPGl. 11. 5.

vohunąm W. Yt. 21. 1 ; Yt.
(APZ.) 23. 8. Cf. *frāyō°*.

vohū Dd. 79. 7 ; Dk. 9. 3. 1 ;
FD. 7 ; Māh Yt. 0 ; N. 20
(3), 37, 39, 46 (6), 47 (3),
48, 84, 109 ; Pl. (5) ; Phl.
Vd. 9. 32, 57 ; 17. 7, 9 ; 19.
18, 47 ; Phl. Ys. 20. 1 ; T.
113 ; W. 1. 1, 2 ; 9. 1 ; W.
Yt. 21. 3, 11 (Haug), 13
(Haug) ; Yt. (APZ.) 23. 8 ;
Yt. (Vtp.) 24. 5, 12, 22, 23,
33, 39, 44, 52, 65. Cf.
ašəm vohū.

vohū-jīti Yt. (APZ.) 23. 1.

vohūmanō A. 12.

vō Yt. (APZ.) 23. 5 ; Yt. (Vtp.)
24, 7, 8 ; ZPGl. 3, 10 ; 13.
3 ; 22. 3.

vōiɣne Phl. Vd. 1. 3 (v. l.
vōɣne).

vōū Phl. Ys. 48 end (Sp.) for
vōhū.

vōhu N. 28.

vōhugaonəm ZPGl. 6. 8.

vōhū Māh Yt. 5 ; N. 14, 20
(3), 34, 35, 46 (6) ; Pars. p.
535 (2) ; Phl. Ys. 27 end
(2), 28 end, 29 end, 30 end,
31 end, 32 end, 33 end, 34
end, 41. 17, 42 end, 43 end,
44 end, 45 end, 46 end, 47
end, 48 end, 49 end, 53 end,
58. 12, 61 end, 64 end, 67
end ; Vij. p. 79, 89, 98, 128,
151, 152, 153, 154 (2), 162,
164 (2), 165 ; ZPGl. 23. 2.

vå N. 70 ; Phl. Ys. 67. 56 (Sp.).

vånha cf. *s°*.

vąθwa Yt. (Vtp.) 24. 38 ; ZPGl.
23. 2.

vnaiti T. 94.

vyāxanąm ZPGl. 18. 6.

vyāxtihava ZPGl. 5. 4.

vyāxnanąm Yt. (Vtp.) 24. 6.

vyāxnəm Yt. (APZ.) 23. 3.

vyādas[*ča* T. 89.

vyānīš T. 63.

vyāzdayå A. 81. (v. l. *vayāzai-
ðyå* and *vayāzdyå*).

vyusō Yt. 22. 7, 25 ; Yt. (Vtp.)
24. 55.

vyåðå N. 69.

vranō Vij. p. 181.

s.

saiti Phl. Vd. 7. 52 (read *hąm-
yāsaiti*).

saite ZPGl. 25. 9 (R. *vaite*).

saiðe ZPGl. 25. 9 (R. *vaiðe*).

sairimananąm Yt. (Vtp.) 24. 52.

saē ZPGl. 5. 7.

saokantahe N. 47.

saokantahe [*ča* W. 5. 1.

saokantəm N. 47; W. 5. 2.

saokavantəm Yt. (Vtp.) 24. 4.

saočantaṭ cf. *a°*.

saočaya [*ča* Yt. 22. 13; Yt. (Vtp.) 24. 37, 59.

saočayanta Yt. (Vtp.) 24. 36.

saočayantaēibyō Vij. p. 127.

saočinavantəm Yt. (APZ.) 23. 6.

saosunčayō Phl. Vd. 8. 74.

saošyantas [*ča* T. 76.

saošyantəm Yt. (Vtp.) 24. 15.

saošyantō W. 4. 1.

saošyantąm Vij. p. 89.

saošyą̊s Yt. (Vtp.) 24. 30.

saxti ZPGl. 26. 3.

saxšəntəm Yt. (Vtp.) 24. 52.

sačaiti N. 50. Cf. *pairi°*.

sata cf. *satōtəmō°*.

sataota Vij. p. 177.

satayārə Yt. (Vtp.) 24. 45.

satavaēsa Yt. (Vtp.) 24. 38.

satavīsahe N. 47.

satāiš Yt. (Vtp.) 24. 19.

satəm W. Yt. 21. 5, 8; Yt. (Vtp.) 24. 13.

satōtəmō-sata Yt. (Vtp.) 24. 19.

sadayaṭ ZPGl. 26. 5.

sadayāṭ N. 65.

sadayeiti Yt. (Vtp.) 24. 1.

saδayeiti Yt. 22. 7 (3), 8, 9, 25 (3), 26; Yt. (Vtp.) 24. 55 (3), 56.

saδayemi Yt. 22. 12.

saδayehi Yt. 22. 11; Yt. (APZ.) 23. 1.

saδōtanąm N. 26.

saδre Yt. (Vtp.) 24. 9.

saṭ-vāstrahe N. 31 (read *is°*).

saŋhaṭ ZPGl. 26. 7 (R. *v°*).

saŋhas [*ča* N. 92.

saŋhahe cf. *nairyō°*.

saŋhāni Yt. (Vtp.) 24. 13.

saŋhəm Yt. (Vtp.) 24. 40; ZPGl. 8. 6, 8; 26. 7.

saŋhō cf. *guδrā°*.

saŋhąn [*ča* cf. *afra°*.

[*saŋhąm*] v. l. N. 37.

sara cf. *aša°*.

sarasčantiš Yt. (Vtp.) 24. 35.

sarəδa N. 47; Phl. Vd. 5. 19; Vij. p. 160; ZPGl. 17. 3.

sarəδaēibyō N. 47.

sarəδanąm [*ča* N. 47.

sarəδahe W. 8. 1.

sarəδō Vij. p. 157.

sarəδyō W. 9. 1.

sareide N. 7.

savavā̊ T. 68.

savō T. 68. Cf. *zavanō°*.

sasti [*ča* N. 46.

sastiš ZPGl. 27. 4.

sahəθrəm T. 50 (read *saxəδrəm*).

sāčayantəm T. 15; Yt. (Vtp.) 24. 52.

sādrā T. 84.

sāδayantiš [*ča* N. 95.

sāyaēti FD. 7.

sārahe N. 42.

sāvaŋhə̄ē N. 61; Phl. Ys. 27 end.

sāsəvištå A. 59.

sāstayāi cf. *duš-həm°* and *huš-həm°*.

sāstra [*ča* Vij. p. 148.

sāsnanąm Yt. (Vtp.) 24. 13.

sāsnå ZPGl. 9. 9.

sāsnås [*ča* T. 4.

sāzdūm T. 6.

sixšəntəm T. 15.

sidaranąm N. 100.

siðiaṯ ZPGl. 26. 1.

sīsraya Yt. (Vtp.) 24. 51.

sukurəna Phl. Vd. 5. 31.

sukəm T. 71 ; ZPGl. 25. 10.

suča ZPGl. 25. 9.

sutəm N. 92.

sunō N. 59.

sura ZPGl. 6. 9.

surahe ZPGl. 16. 7.

surunaoiti Yt. 22. 41.

surunaōiti N. 21.

surunuyå N. 69.

surunv- cf. *aiwi°*.

surunvaiti N. 27.

surunvainti N. 24.

surunvanti N. 20.

surąm ZPGl. 42. 10. Cf. *ušąm°*.

suši ZPGl. 10. 10.

sūnahe Yt. (Vtp.) 24. 44.

sūnō T. 9 ; Vij. p. 87.

sūra Yt. (Vtp.) 24. 46.

sūrahe N. 47 (2) ; W. 5. 1.

sūrəm N. 47 ; W. 5. 2.

sūrō T. 103 (2).

sūrå ZPGl. 26. 8.

sūš FD. 3.

səvištəm N. 61.

səvišta ZPGl. 25. 10.

səvištō N. 35 ; Phl. Ys. 27 end ; Yt. (APZ.) 23. 2.

səvištå cf. *sā°*.

sōinma N. 100.

såṇha ZPGl. 26. 5 (R. *v°*).

sącaδ [*ča* N. 81.

sąsaṇhąm Phl. Vd. 2. 10.

skarənayå A. 66.

skəndō W. 8. 2.

sčaēniš N. 58.

sčindayaṯ ZPGl. 26. 1.

staoiti W. Yt. 21. 3 (2), 9, 11, 13, 15. Cf. *upa.°*

staota N. 37 ; Vij. p. 89, 148.

staotanąm Yt. (Vtp.) 24. 28.

staotaras [*ča* N. 34.

staotəm W. 1. 1.

staomaidi N. 48.

staomaide N. 48 ; Vij. p. 165, 166 ; W. 7. 2.

staomā [*ča* CB.

staomi Pars. p. 521 ; Vij. p. 141.

staomī N. 46 (3).

staorəm N. 45.

staōta T. 21.

[*staōṇhaiti*] v. l. N. 42.

staxtō ZPGl. 26. 4.

staxrahe W. 8. 2.

staxrō W. 8. 2 ; ZPGl. 26. 4.

staṇhas [*ča* cf. *variš°*.

stayāṯ N. 63.

star- cf. *a°* and *fra°*.

starəm T. 38.

staryeti N. 10.

stavaṇhō N. 90.

stavanō Phl. Vd. **7.** 43

stavå cf. *gāu°*.

stāta ZPGl. 26. 3.

stār- cf. *ā°*.

stārō Ep. M. **1.** 4. 3 ; N. 47 ;
Pars. p. 535 ; Vij. p. 136.

stārą̇m ZPGl. 12. 8.

stāhyanąm Yt. (Vtp.) **24.** 6.

sti N. 83.

stiδāta Phl. Vd. **2.** 40.

[*stimyazdōiš*] v. l. N. 83.

stiš Phl. Vd. **2.** 19.

stuiuxtiš N. 79.

stuiti ZPGl. 19. 1.

stutō W. Yt. **21.** 2.

stuye cf. *a°*.

stūiti cf. *apa°*, *ašō°*, *āš°*, and
upa.

stūna Phl. Ys. **9.** 4. Cf. *bǝrǝzi°·*

stǝnbya ZPGl. 26. 4.

stǝraiti N. 103.

stǝrǝnaēiti N. 102.

stǝrǝnōiti T. 38.

stǝrǝnti N. 103.

stǝreiti cf. *barǝsmō°*.

stǝhr-paēsaṇhǝm Vij. p. 180.

stǝhr-paēsaṇhō Vij. p. 160.

stē-rapantąm Yt. (Vtp.) **24.** 6
(2).

stōiš N. 47 (2), 81 ; Phl. Ys.
67. 51 (Sp.) ; ZPGl. 40. 8.

stå̇ṇhaiti N. 42.

strayą̇s[*ča* cf. *urvarō°*.

stri ZPGl. 26. 1.

strīm ZPGl. **5.** 4.

strǝnti N. 95, 96.

strą̇m cf. *urvarō°*.

stry- cf. *a°*.

spaiti Yt. (Vtp.) **24.** 35.

spaxštīm ZPGl. 26. 1. Cf.
pouru°.

spanvanti W. Yt. **21.** 4.

spayaθrahe W. **8.** 2.

spayama cf. *ava°*.

spayeiti N. 11 ; Phl. Vd. **3.** 42
(4).

spayōiš cf. *fra°*.

sparōiṯ Yt. (Vtp.) **24.** 35.

sparṇha ZPGl. **8.** 4.

sparmaini Yt. (Vtp.) **24.** 36.

spasanya N. 8.

spānahe Phl. Vd. **13.** 48.

spitama Ep. M. **1.** 4. 3 (2) ; Yt.
(Vtp.) **24.** 65.

spitama zaraθuštra A. 51 ; N.
84 (3) ; Phl. Vd. **7.** 52 (2) ; T.
45, 108 ; Vij. p. 23, 25, 139,
141, 145, 181 ; W. **4.** 1, 2,
3 ; W. Yt. **21.** 5 ; Yt. (Vtp.)
24. 29.

spitamahe Vij. p. 128.

spitami zaraθuštra Vij. p. 180.

spitamō (*i*) *zaraθuštrō* Vij. p.
138.

spitāmǝm zaraθuštrǝm Vij. p.
126.

spitāmō Yt. (APZ.) **23.** 4.

spǝtama zaraθuštra T. 13, 32,
47, 64, 66, 78, 87, 90, 91,
94.

spənta N. 20, 28, 46, 65, 71, 102; VS. Extr. 4; Vij. p. 54 [*s(a)pənta*], 128; Yt. (Vtp.) **24**. 32.

spəntaēibyō Phl. Vd. **19**. 25.

spəntaṯ Yt. **22**. 40.

spəntanąm CB; Pars. p. 535; Vij. p. 141, 181; W. **1**. 2; **5**. 1; Yt. (Vtp.) **24**. 46.

spəntama zaraθuštra T. 99.

spəntamahe N. 46.

spəntayå Vij. p. 184.

spəntas[*ča* Yt. (Vtp.) **24**. 47.

spəntahe Pars. p. 535; VS. Extr. 3; Yt. **22**. 38 (3); Yt. (Vtp.) **24**. 28, 51.

spəntā N. 34, 46, 47, 50, 102 (2); Phl. Ys. **46** end, **47** end, **48** end, **49** end; SlS. **13**. 1; Vij. p. 152; W. **5**. 2; Yt. (Vtp.) **24**. 40.

spəntāi VS. Extr. 1.

spənti N. 101.

spəntəm Pars. p. 531; VS. Extr. 2.

spəntə̄ N. 70; T. 76; Yt. (Vtp.) **24**. 12.

spəntō N. ˙47; W. **9**. 1; Yt. (Vtp.) **24**. 49.

spəntō-dātāi Yt. (Vtp.) **24**. 25.

spəntå T. 102; Vij. p. 12.

spəntąm Pars. p. 534; Yt. (Vtp.) **24**. 50.

spərəza ZPGl. **10**. 11.

spə̄ništa W. Yt. **21**. 1; Yt. **22**. 1.

spå̄nta cf. *gao°*.

spnāθrəm] T.' 49 (read *xšnao-θrəm*).

snaiθiš T. 33, 35.

snaēθiša T. 6.

snaoδō-manå Yt. (Vtp.) **24**. 31.

snaoδō-vačå Yt. (Vtp.) **24**. 31.

snaoδō-š[*y*]*aoθnå* Yt. (Vtp.) **24**. 31.

snaθahe W. **8**. 2.

snaθāi Pars. p. 534 (3), 535.

snaθənti cf. *dōiə̄°*.

snayehi cf. *fra°*.

snākəniš[*ča* N. 57.

snātō ZPGl. **26**. 6.

snāvarə ZPGl. **26**. 6.

snus ZPGl. **26**. 6.

syāvaršānō Yt. (APZ.) **23**. 3.

sraēšta[*ča* N. 84.

sraēštāiš Yt. **22**. 9; Yt. (Vtp.) **24**. 56.

sraēštąm Pars. p. 531; Yt. **22**. 10; Yt. (Vtp.) **24**. 57.

sraota Yt. (Vtp.) **24**. 31.

sraota-gaošąm Yt. (Vtp.) **24**. 14.

sraotanvō Yt. **22**. 9; Yt. (Vtp.) **24**. 56.

sraotaranąm N. 21.

sraotarō N. 21.

sraotārō N. 21 (2). Cf. *upa°*.

sraoθrana N. 22.

sraoθrəm Yt. (Vtp.) **24**. 53.

sraoθrå N. 44.

sraoni ZPGl. **10**. 12.

sraoni-maså ZPGl. **39**. 7.

sraošahe N. 61 (2) ; Vij. p. 157.

sraošāvarǝzahe N. 79; Yt. (Vtp.) **24**. 15.

sraošāvarǝzǝm N. 82.

sraošāvarǝzō N. 77.

sraoši N. 7.

sraošǝm Phl. Ys. **27** end ; T. 70; Yt. (APZ.) **23**. 6 ; ZPGl. 9. 4.

sraošǝm [*ča* Yt. (Vtp.) **24**. 14, 40.

sraošō Phl. Vd. **18**. 14 ; Vij. p. 126, 139.

sraošō-čaranaya T. 8.

sraošyanąm cf. *a°*.

sraxtim N. 79 (2).

sraɣrǝm ZPGl. 20. 10.

sraya Yt. (Vtp.) **24**. 56.

* *srayana* [*ča* T. 94 (so for *θr°*).

srayana [*ča* W. Yt. **21**. 6, 8, 10, 12, 14, 16 ; Yt. **22**. 11.

srayanō Yt. (Vtp.) **24**. 36.

srayas [*ča* Yt. (Vtp.) **24**. 58.

srayā̊ Yt. **22**. 9.

srava cf. *hu°*.

sravaṯ ZPGl. 26. 6.

sravaṅh- cf. *hao°*.

sravaṅhǝm N. 22.

sravaṅhąm W. **4**. 1 (2).

sravay- cf. *a°* and *fra°*.

sravayōiṯ N. 48.

sravārō Vij. p. 138.

sravō T. 20.

srasčintǝm cf. *a°*.

srāyamnō N. 23.

srāyeiti N. 37.

srāvananąm [*ča* N. 83.

srāvamnąm N. 22.

srāvayaṯ N. 85.

srāvayanti N. 32.

srāvayantō N. 25.

srāvayeiti N. 26, 29, 31, 46.

srāvayeiðyāi Yt. (Vtp.) **24**. 46.

srāvayǝnti N. 31.

srāvayō N. 22, 27 ; Yt. **22**. 2, 13, 20 ; Yt. (Vtp.) **24**, 54, 59.

srāvayōiṯ N. 46, 50, 109 ; Vij. p. 166 ; W. **7**. 2.

srāvayōiš T. 11, 21.

srāvayti N. 50.

srāsayā̊ cf. *u°*.

srita ZPGl. 26. 8.

sritō N. 78.

srišaiti N. 99.

srišāiti N. 99.

[*srīm*] v. l. N. 65.

srīra Phl. Vd. **2**. 10 ; Yt. (Vtp.) **24**. 22 ; ZPGl. 8. 6.

srīrayā̊ Yt. **22**. 9 ; Yt. (Vtp.) **24**. 56.

srīrā Yt. (Vtp.) **24**. 33.

srīrǝm N. 65 ; Vij. p. 180, 181 ; Yt. (APZ.) **23**. 3 ; Yt. (Vtp.) **24**. 28, 33 ; ZPGl. 9. 3.

srīrōtarąm Yt. **22**. 14 ; Yt. (Vtp.) **24**. 60.

srīrā̊ ZPGl. 26. 2.

srīrąm Yt. **22**. 14 ; Yt. (Vtp.) **24**. 60.

sruiti cf. (*ā*) *fra°*.

sruta ZPGl. 26. 2.

srutanąm N. 37.

srutəm cf. *dūraē°*.

srutō-gāθå N. 25.

sruṭ ct. *həm°*.

srunaoiti ZPGl. 26. 7.

srūmi Phl. Ys. 64. 48 (Sp.) v. l. *ahasrīma*.

srvatō ZPGl. 26. 3.

svō ZPGl. 25. 10.

š.

šaitō ZPGl. 18. 12.

šaētavaitanąm Vij. p. 158.

šaētō Vth. 5, 15 ; ZPGl. 18. 12.

šaota Yt. (Vtp.) 24. 26.

šaoθananąm Phl. Ys. 19. 13.

šaoθnå cf. *snaoδō°*.

šaošaiti ZPGl. 19. 4.

šaθąm Phl. Vd. 1. 2.

šaninąm Vij. p. 138.

šamąn T. 7.

šāuō N. 67.

šātəm T. 44, 74.

šātōiš Yt. 22. 2, 4, 6.   Cf. *a°* and *dī°*.

šātō-manå A. 3.

šāma ZPGl. 11. 2.

šāvayeiti N. 103.

šāvayōiṭ N. 46.

šieiti ZPGl. 18. 13.

šitibyas[*ča* Yt. 22. 16, 34 ; Yt. (Vtp.) 24. 62.

šuąs ZPGl. 36. 4.

šutasme ZPGl. 19. 2.

šuδəm ZPGl. 19. 2.

šustəm ZPGl. 19. 2.

šənəm ZPGl. 19. 3.

šē N. 7, 17, 42, 105 ; T. 55 ; Yt. (Vtp.) 24. 28.   Cf. *paiti-šē*.

šoiθrō ZPGl. 18. 10.

šōiθrəm T. 5.

šōθna[*ča* T. 58.

šå N. 101.

štačaṭ cf. *gāθwō°*.

štāitya cf. *išarə°*.

šnaoθna Yt. (Vtp.) 24. 40.

šyaoθana N. 67 ; Vij. p. 25.   Cf. *duš°* and *hu°*.

šyaoθananąm N. 16, 46 (3), 48.

šyaoθanəm A. 27 ; N. 42.

šyaoθanəm[*ča* N. 29.

šyaoθanō-tāitya N. 81.

šyaoθnā N. 22.

šyaoθ̄nanąm Vij. p. 67, 151.

šyaōθnaṭ cf. *hu°*.

šyaoθnanąm Phl. Vd. 7. 52.

šyātō ZPGl. 18. 12.

z.

zaini-paršta VS. Extr. 4.

zaini-parštahe VS. Extr. 3.

zaini-parštāi VS. Extr. 1.

zaini-parštəm VS. Extr. 2.

zainti cf. *fra°*.

zaintyas[*ča* cf. *paiti°*.

zairimyāka Phl. Vd. 13. 6, 7.

zaēnaṇha ZPGl. 30. 6.

zaēmanō ZPGl. 16. 6.
zaēšō ZPGl. 30. 6.
zaota N. 20, 21 (3), 38, 39 (3), 70, 80 (2), 81 ; Pl.
zaotara N. 78.
zaotara[*ča* Vij. p. 134.
zaotarō N. 21.
zaotarš N. 72, 81 (2).
zaotā Māh Yt. o ; N. 37 (3).
zaoθa N. 33.
zaoθra ZPGl. 30. 3.
zaoθraδa N. 40.
zaoθranąm N. 83, 84.
zaoθranąm[*ča* Vij. p. 89.
zaoθraya N. 57.
zaoθras[*ča* N. 73.
zaoθrāṯ N. 65.
zaoθrābyō N. 46, 71 ; Vij. p. 127; Yt. 22. 38; ZPGl. 17. 1.
zaoθrəm N. 80. Cf. *haδa°*.
zaoθre N. 68.
zaoθrō-barana N. 66.
zaoθrå N. 65, 68, 71 ; T. 36.
zaoθrąm N. 46, 48, 64 (4); Phl. Vd. 3. 14.
zaoδa N. 21.
zaoyehe Phl. Vd. 1. 14.
zaošō ZPGl. 30. 3.
zagaθaṯ ZPGl. 30. 7 (R. *gaθaṯ*).
zatō N. 97 ; ZPGl. 30. 9.
zad T. 20 (read *yaṯ*).
zaṇhəm N. 65.
zanta ZPGl. 30. 4.
zantaoṯ N. 8.
zantavō T. 22.
zantu-baxtəm T. 95.

zantu-patōiš Yt. (Vtp.) 24. 16.
zantōuš Yt. (Vtp.) 24. 16.
zantōuš[*ča* N. 8.
zantvō N. 8.
zaya W. 8. 2.
zavana Phl. Vd. 1. 3 ; 2. 41.
zayāiti Vth. 4, 9.
zayāṯ Phl. Ys. 10. 1, 3.
zayene N. 61.
zayånte Yt. (APZ.) 23. 5 ; Yt. (Vtp.) 24. 1, 3. Cf. *us°*.
zaraθuštra A. 51 ; Ep. M. 1. 4. 3 (2); FD. 3 ; HtN. p. 483, 485 ; Phl. Vd. 5. 2 ; 7. 52 (2); 18. 2 ; T. 13, 32, 45, 47, 55, 58, 60, 64, 66, 78, 87, 90, 91, 94, 98, 99, 103, 105, 108; Vij. p. 23, 25, 139, 141, 180, 181 ; W. 1. 2 ; 4. 2 ; 8. 2 ; W. Yt. 21. 2, 4, 5, 7, 9, 11, 13, 15, 17 ; Yt. 22. 20, 25, 40 ; Yt. (Vtp.) 24. 1 (2), 8, 10, 11 (2), 12, 28 (2), 29, 32, 34, 37, 42 (2), 43, 48 ; ZPGl. 15. 3.
zaraθuštrahe v. l. FD. 4 ; N. 46 ; T. 120 ; Vij. p. 128 ; W. 1. 1.
zaraθuštrāi VS. Extr. 1.
zaraθuštri N. 33 ; VS. Extr. 2, 4.
zaraθuštriš N. 58, 103.
zaraθuštrəm Phl. Ys. 10. 1, 3 ; Vij. p. 126.
zaraθuštrəš N. 20.

zaraθuštrō N. 63 ; Vij. p. 53, 138 ; Vth. 1 ; W. Yt. 21. 1 ; Yt. 22. 1, 19 ; Yt. (APZ.) 23. 1, 4 ; Yt. (Vtp.) 24. 2, 6, 10, 22, 24, 40, 65.

zaraθuštrōiš N. 2, 31 ; VS. Extr. 3.

zaraðaγnyāi [*ča* Phl. Vd. 1. 14.

zaranim A. 84.

zaranumatō Yt. (Vtp.) 24. 4.

zaranumantəm Yt. (Vtp.) 24. 4.

zaranyō A. 17.

zaranyō-kərətō A. 12.

zarazdātōiṭ T. 62 ; W. Yt. 21. 3.

zarahe T. 41.

zarāðvehe Vij. p. 138.

zarətəm Phl. Vd. 3. 14 ; T. 38.

zarəðaēm Phl. Vd. 1. 3.

zarənumantəm N. 47 ; W. 5. 2.

zarənumantō N. 47 ; W. 5. 1.

zarəmaya cf. *maiðyōi°*.

zarəmayehe A. 16 ; Yt. 22. 18 ; Yt. (Vtp.) 24. 64.

zarəsō cf. *a°*.

zarōnəm Yt. (APZ.) 23. 4.

zarva ZPGl. 30. 5.

zarvānəm [*ča* ZPGl. 13. 11.

zarštay- cf. *hu°*.

[*zava*] v. l. FD. 3.

zavanō-savō Yt. (Vtp.) 24. 8.

zavarus [*ču* ZPGl. 17. 5.

zavarə [*ča* Pars. p. 522.

zavavaṭ Yt. (Vtp.) 24. 30.

zasta Vij. p. 133 ; Yt. (Vtp.) 24. 31 ; ZPGl. 10. 3 ; 30. 1.

zastaēibya A. 27 ; Vij. p. 139.

zastaēibyō Phl. Vd. 2. 32.

zastayas [*ča* T. 57.

zastavaṭ ZPGl. 30. 1.

zastō cf. *ustāna°*.

[*zazuš*] v. l. FD. 3.

zazuša FD. 3 and v. l.

zazušu T. 56 (2).

zazva FD. 3 (2).

[*zahmi*] v. l. FD. 3.

zā ZPGl. 12. 7.

zāta N. 97.

zātanąm cf. *kuðō°*.

zātayå cf. *ā°*.

zāniti FD. 7.

zāmaoiō ZPGl. 30. 6.

zāyōš [*ča* N. 57 (v. l. *zyāiš°*).

zārayōiš cf. *ā°*.

zāras [*ča* ZPGl. 10. 11.

zāvarə Phl. Ys. 64. 48 (Sp.) ; ZPGl. 30. 4.

zāvarə [*ča* Pars. p. 532.

zi N. 68 ; SkN. p. 480 ; Yt. 22. 39.

zü N. 68.

zita ZPGl. 30. 2.

zinda ZPGl. 30. 9.

zimahe Phl. Vd. 1. 3 (2). Cf. *hazaṃrō°*.

zirijå A. 57.

zī A. 49 ; Dk. (P. Sj.) 3. p. 131 ; Ep. M. 1. 4. 3 (2) ; N.

22, 46, 84 ; Phl. Vd. 4. 10 ;
T. 18, 22, 25, 28, 32, 37, 69,
91, 98, 112 ; Vij. p. 181 ;
W. 4. 1 ; 8. 1, 2 ; 9 ; W. Yt.
21. 4, 5 ; Yt. (Vtp.) 24. 11,
12, 28, 29, 30, 36 ; ZPGl.
30. 1.
zīmana N. 17.
zīzušte cf. *ā°*.
zurō-bərətå ZPGl. 30. 7.
zuša ZPGl. 30. 2.
zušta Phl. Vd. 17. 9 ; ZPGl.
30. 3.
zuštō ZPGl. 43. 10.
zəṅha ZPGl. 11. 4.
zəngō cf. *arədvō°*.
zəm N. 101.
zəmaēnaēibya N. 107.
zəmana ZPGl. 30. 5.
zəmar-gūzō W. 4. 3 (2).
zəme Phl. Vd. 2. 32 ; 3. 40.
zəmō A. 66 ; Phl. Vd. 2. 32 ;

3. 40 ; 9. 32 (2) ; Vij. p.
116 ; ZPGl. 18. 9 ; 40. 6.
zərəðaiem ZPGl. 30. 8.
z∂naṅhutəm Yt. (APZ.) 23. 2.
zą̇θəm [*ča* Yt. (Vtp.) 24. 49.
zą̇θwa ZPGl. 30. 5.
zą̇m Phl. Vd. 5. 7 ; Vij. p. 57 ;
W. Yt. 21. 3, 16 (2) ; Yt. 22.
20 ; Yt. (Vtp.) 24. 65.
zgərəgnəm ZPGl. 30. 7.
ztayå Yt. 22. 9.
zbaya- cf. *upa°*.
zbayaiša cf. *ni°*.
zman [*a*]*yå* N. 17.
[*zyaiš* [*ča*] v. l. N. 57.
zyeiṯ ZPGl. 39. 2.
zyą̇m ZPGl. 30. 2.
zru N. 12.
zrva ZPGl. 30. 5.
zrvānahe Yt. (Vtp.) 24. 24.
zrvānəm Phl. Vd. 2. 19 ; T. 79.
zrvō-dātanąm Yt. (Vtp.) 24. 27.

ž.

žintəm cf. *varō°*.
žəntəm Yt. (Vtp.) 24. 59.

žnātō cf. *hupaitī°*.
žnum ZPGl. 11. 3.

h.

haita ZPGl. 32. 2.
haiti ZPGl. 32. 1.
haitīm Phl. Vd. 1. 1 ; Yt. 22.
14 (3).
haiθi N. 84 ; ZPGl. 32. 1.
haiθīm ZPGl. 12. 6.
haiθəm- vačå ZPGl. 8. 9.
haiθyə̄m Phl. Ys. 27 end.

haiθyå W. 9. 2.
hourva N. 37.
haurvata N. 28 (3).
haurvatātəm Vij. p. 52.
haurvatātō N. 47.
haurvaṯbya W. Yt. 21. 7.
haurvī T. 64.
haurvō N. 63.

hauštuayå T. 61.

haē N. 79.

haē[*čā* W. 8. 2.

haēbvant Phl. Ys. 38. 7 (Sp.).
　Av?

haēna ZPGl. 32. 4.

haēnayå A. 81.

haoiδ ZPGl. 9. 11.

haourvō N. 20.

haotəmāi N. 70.

haom Ht. N. p. 486; Vij. p.
　179 (2).

haoma Māh Yt. 5; N. 46 (2).

haomanąm N. 46.

haomavaitanąm[*ča* Vij. p. 89.

haomavaitibyō Vij. p. 127.

haomavaitīm N. 46.

haomahe N. 46; W. Yt. 21. 9.

haomāi N. 46; Vij. p. 99.

haoməm N. 46 (2).

haoməm[*ča* N. 72, 75 (2), 76.

haomō N. 46.

haomąn N. 68.

haomąs[*ča* N. 97.

haomya N. 108.

haomyąm N. 48, 79.

haoyāṯ N. 79.

haosravaŋhəm ZPGl. 11. 10.

haosravaŋhe ZPGl. 31. 10.

haosravaŋhāi Yt. (Vtp.) 24. 32.

haōnā T. 39 (read *hāu nā*).

haōnəm T. 60 (read *haoməm*).

haōm Vij. p. 25.

haōmanaŋhəm T. 73.

hakaṯ N. 24 (2); SlS. 8. 22;
　ZPGl. 3. 2.

hakarəṯ N. 41.

hakərəṯ ZPGl. 2. 11.

haxa ZPGl. 31. 10.

haxaδra Yt. (Vtp.) 24. 10.

haxaδrāi Yt. (Vtp.) 24. 34.

haxaδre Yt. (Vtp.) 24. 31.

haxaya Yt. (Vtp.) 24. 10.

haxəδre Yt. (Vtp.) 24. 43.

haxəm ZPGl. 11. 4.

haxta ZPGl. 10. 12.

haxti Phl. Vd. 8. 58.

haxtō N. 6, 80.

haxtōiṯ N. 9.

haxšaēte N. 9.

haxšōiṯ Yt. (Vtp.) 24. 38.

haγδaŋhəm Yt. (Vtp.) 24. 38.

hača A. 12, 19, 58; CB; N.
　4, 8, 41, 42, 46 (2), 47, 48,
　49 (2), 50 (2), 51, 54, 61,
　62, 83; Phl. Vd. 1. 18; 19.
　41; T. 32, 39, 59 (2), 62,
　67; Vij. p. 24, 25 (2), 145,
　181; Vth. 4, 9; W. 3. 2;
　W. Yt. 21. 3; Yt. 22. 7 (2),
　16 (2), 25 (2), 34 (4), 40, 42
　(2); Yt. (APZ.) 23. 5; Yt.
　(Vtp.) 24. 15, 27, 29, 62 (4).

hačaiti Vij. p. 127. Cf. *paraŋ°*.

hačaite ZPGl. 13. 1.

hačatu Yt. (Vtp.) 24. 8.

hačaṯ-aēšąm Yt. (Vtp.) 24. 14.

hačaṯ-paēmanyąm Yt. (Vtp.) 24.
　13, 49.

hačaṯ-puθrąm Yt. (Vtp.) 24. 13,
　49.

hačanuha N. 9.

hačayāṯ Yt. (Vtp.) 24. 47.

hačā N. 41, 46 (2), 60, 67, 102 (2); T. 31, 114.

hačimnō W. 1. 1.

hatąm HtN. p. 483; Phl. Vd. 3. 31.

haθwa[*ča* Yt. (Vtp.) 24. 46.

haθra N. 7, 59; Yt. (Vtp.) 24. 39, 42.

haθrayən Yt. (Vtp.) 24. 42.

haθra(*čiš*) N. 100, 101.

haθrākəm N. 4.

haθrāknəm N. 2.

haθrānivāitīm Yt. (Vtp.) 24. 25.

haθrem[*čiṯ* N. 109.

haθrånčō N. 88.

haθrąm W. 9. 2.

had- cf. *nišāδayōiš* and *nišhid-*.

haδa Vij. p. 116, 127 (2), 145 (2), 181 (2); ZPGl. 3. 1; 32. 1.

haδaoxδāi N. 61.

haδa-dāta VS. Extr. 4.

haδa-dātahe VS. Extr. 3.

haδa-dātāi VS. Extr. 1.

haδa-dātəm VS. Extr. 2.

haδaṇhrō ZPGl. 32. 5, 6.

haδa-mąθra VS. Extr. 4.

haδa-mąθrahe VS. Extr. 3.

haδa-mąθrāi VS. Extr. 1.

haδa-mąθrəm VS. Extr. 2.

haδa-zaoθrəm N. 46.

haδā-naēpatavaitīm N. 46.

haδō N. 59.

haδō-gaēθanąm N. 60.

hapō-gaēθa N. 1 (read *haδō°*).

hapta N. 102; Phl. Vd. 1. 3; 2. 41; Vij. p. 160; ZPGl. 18. 7.

haptaθa N. 102.

haptaθəm N. 82.

haptaṇhāitīm N. 46, 65, 80.

haptaṇhum ZPGl. 1. 8.

hapsnāi-apnō-xavō ZPGl. 5. 6. (R. reads *hapsne°*.)

haṇhāma ZPGl. 11. 6.

haṇhuharəne ZPGl. 10. 1.

hana N̥. 9; ZPGl. 5. 8.

hanaire Yt. (Vtp.) 24. 31, 34.

hanairyāi Yt. (Vtp.) 24. 43.

hanā[*ča* Yt. (Vtp.) 24. 28.

hanāṯ W. 9. 1.

hankanayən Phl. Vd. 9. 32 (2).

hankārayaēmi ZPGl. 32. 5.

hankərəθyąm cf. *vīspō°*.

hangərəfāṯ N. 65.

[*hangərəftāṯ*] v. l. N. 65.

hanjamanəm Vij. p. 158.

hanjasaiti N. 43.

hanjasanta N. 42.

hanjasante N. 62.

hanjasånte N. 65.

hantačinå Yt. (Vtp.) 24. 49.

ha� hantō N. 53.

handaraite T. 19.

handaramana N. 53.

handarəžanti N. 101.

handāitīm Yt. (Vtp.) 24. 29.

handāta N. 102; Yt. (Vtp.) 24 28; ZPGl. 32. 4.

handātā N. 102.

handərəxti ZPGl. 34. 8.

handvaraiti Yt. 22. 20.

hama N. 46, 48, 50, 51, 94, 103; v. l. Phl. Vd. 7. 4; SkN. p. 480; ZPGl. 38. 6.

hamaēθə̄ v. l. (D. note) A. 81.

hamaθa N. 47.

hamayå SlS. 13. 43.

hamaraθanąm Yt. (Vtp.) 24. 19.

hamartə̄ Yt. (Vtp.) 24. 6.

[*hamas*[*čiţ*] v. l. for *aməša°*.

hamaspaθmaiδəm Vij. p. 184.

hamaspaθmaēdaya AG. 10.

hamahe Yt. (Vtp.) 24. 41.

hamərəθanąm Yt. (Vtp.) 24. 25.

hamō N. 64.

hamō-varəšajim N. 98.

hamąm N. 64 (6).

harəta ZPGl. 31. 10.

harəθraēibyō N. 85.

harəθrīm cf. *nišaṇ°*.

harəθrəm Vij. p. 24, 25.

harəštəe cf. *upari°*.

harəšyanti N. 46.

harəšyamnanąm N. 46.

harəzāţ cf. *upaṇ°* and *paiti°*.

harōiţ cf. *fraṇ°*.

hava N. 84 (2), 108; T. 35, 101; Yt. 22. 9, 11 (2); Yt. (Vtp.) 24. 42, 58.

havaēibya N. 27, 108.

havatąm N. 13.

havaţ N. 68.

havapaṇhāi Phl. Ys. 38. 8 (Sp.).

havaṇhəm ZPGl. 11. 10.

havaṇhāi Yt. (Vtp.) 24. 32.

havanaēibya N. 107, 108.

havanəm N. 47.

havanō N. 107.

havanąm W. 4. 2.

havayaṇhəm N. 15.

havara Yt. (Vtp.) 24. 10.

havahe N. 84, 108.

haǫvā N. 55.

havāi A. 49; N. 105.

havō W. 8. 1; Yt. 22. 1, 3, 5, 19; Yt. (Vtp.) 24. 54.

havąm Vij. p. 148; Yt. (Vtp.) 24. 39.

hastarəm N. 31.

hastrəm N. 31 (2).

hazaošyāpaåṇha N. 1 (read *hazaošyā p°*).

hazaṇuha N. 6.

hazaṇra Vij. p. 132.

hazaṇra-yaoxštyō Yt. (APZ.) 23. 3.

hazaṇrahe Vij. p. 97.

hazaṇrāi Yt. (Vtp.) 24. 19.

hazaṇrəm AG. 5, 6, 7, 8, 9; N. 42 (2), 52, 60; W. Yt. 21. 10; Yt. (Vtp.) 24. 5.

hazaṇrōtəmō-hazaṇra Yt. (Vtp.) 24. 19.

hazaṇrō-zimahe Phl. Vd. 2. 19.

hazaṇha N. 63 (2).

hazahīš[*ča* T. 36.

hazō ZPGl. 39. 3.

huhi T. 67.

hahya cf. *paitiš°*.

hā N. 105; Phl. Vd. 19. 30;
W. 8. 2 (2); Yt. (Vtp.) 24.
28.

hāi Yt. (Vtp.) 24. 44.

hāitišu N. 40.

hāitīm Yt. (Vtp.) 24. 60 (2).
Cf. *haptan°*.

hāitīm[ča N. 46

hāirišinąm Yt. (Vtp.) 24. 50.

hāu Ep. M. 1. 4. 3; T. 35, 39
(*haōna*), 47, 103, 104, 105;
W. Yt. 21. 7, 9, 11, 13, 15,
17; Yt. (Vtp.) 24. 47, 48.

hāu[ča T. 45.

hātōiš N. 102 (2).

hātąm N. 65; Pars. p. 532 (2);
Phl. Vd. 3. 31; 18. 51; Phl.
Ys. 21 end; 56. 1, 12; 62
end; 67 end; 70 end; Yt.
(Vtp.) 24. 30.

hāθanąm N. 40.

hāθra N. 97 (read *hāθrakaēbiš*).

hāθrahe N. 11, 60, 104.

hāθrākǝbiš N. 97.

hāθrāčiš N. 100.

hāθrāt̰ N. 104.

hāθrāhe N. 104.

hāθrǝm N. 8, 109; ZPGl. 41.
10; 43. 1, 4.

haθrō N. 11.

hāθrå N. 88.

hāδ- cf. *aspan°* and *niš°*.

hāt̰ N. 11.

hāmō N. 64 (3).

hāmō-nāfō Yt. (Vtp.) 24. 37.

hāra N. 7.

hāvana N. 68, 102; Vij. p.
83 (2).

hāvanaēibyō N. 81.

hāvanayō cf. *pairiš°*.

hāvanānǝm N. 46, 82.

hāvanānō N. 72, 79, 81; Yt.
(Vtp.) 24. 15.

hāvanǝ̄e N. 61 (2); Phl. Ys. 27
end.

[*hāvayāt̰*] v. l. N. 72.

hāvaynāne N. 80.

hikuš ZPGl. 32. 3.

hixšaēša Yt. (Vtp.) 24. 45.

hixšaθa Yt. (Vtp.) 24. 47.

hixšat̰ ZPGl. 32. 3.

hičitā ZPGl. 32. 2.

hita N. 107.

hitō ZPGl. 8. 7.

hiδ- cf. *niš°*.

hit̰ ZPGl. 3. 1.

hinčat̰ ZPGl. 32. 3.

hindūm Phl. Vd. 1. 18.

hindva Phl. Vd. 1. 18 (v. l.
hǝn°).

him N. 3, 42.

hiš N. 4, 28, 55 (2), 108.

hišǝmnō T. 10.

hištat̰ cf. *usǝ°*.

hištanǝmnō N. 37.

hištǝntǻ Yt. (Vtp.) 24. 36.

hišyāta T. 25.

hišyānaōtǝmǝm T. 25.

hizva A. 26; Phl. Vd. 2. 5;
T. 101; Vij. p. 24; ZPGl.
8. 5.

hizvas[ča T. 57.

hizvąm N. 17 ; SlS. **11**. 6 ; T. 3.

hīm FD. 3 ; N. 48 ; Yt. **22**.
    10 ; Yt. (Vtp.) 24. 62.

hīš N. 70 (in *vahehīš*) ; T. 41.

hu N. 48.

huitīm N. 108.

huki N. 95.

hukərəfš ZPGl. 6. 2.

huxta [*ča* W. Yt. **21**. 13, 15.

huxtay- cf. *frāyō°*.

huxtā Ganj. 5, 6 (2) ; Mād-
    ch. 12.

huxšaθrahe T. 9.

huxšaθrā W. **5**. 2.

huxšaθrōtəmāi N. 35.

hugaonəm ZPGl. 6. 6.

hutarəst ZPGl. 6. 4.

hutahe W. Yt. **21**. 9.

hutāštəm W. **5**. 2.

hutāštahe W. **5**. 1.

hutāštō ZPGl. 6. 1.

hudaēna Yt. **22**. 11, 12 ; Yt.
    (Vtp.) 24. 58.

hudaēnaṭ T. 67.

hudaēnahe Yt. **22**. 18 ; Yt.
    (Vtp.) 24. 9, 64.

huðātō N. 46.

huðå N. 28 ; Vij. p. 79.   Cf.
    gaō°.

huðåṇhəm N. 61 ; Yt. (APZ.)
    23. 3.

huðåṇhe Yt. (Vtp.) 24. 41.

huðåṇhō N. 67 ; W. **5**. 2 ; **6**.
    1 (3).

hupaitianātō A. 53 (read *°pai-*
    tiẑnāᵛ).

hupātəm Yt. (Vtp.) 24. 42.

hufərəθwəm T. 72.

hufrāšmō N. 50.

hubaoiðita [*ča* Yt. **22**. 11 ; Yt.
    (Vtp.) 24. 58.

hubaoiðitarō Yt. **22**. 7 ; Yt.
    (Vtp.) 24. 55.

hubaoiðitəməm Yt. **22**. 8 ; Yt.
    (Vtp.) 24. 55.

hubaoiðiš Yt. **22**. 7 ; Yt. (Vtp.)
    24. 55.

hubaðrō A. 53.

hubarāna Yt. (Vtp.) 24. 27.

hubərəitīm [*ča* T. 88.

hubərətīš [*ča* N. 48 ; W. **7**.
    2.

hunarəm T. 78.

hunąm Phl. Vd. **2**. 10, 18.

hunyāṭ N. 58.

humaiti cf. *a°*.

humata Ganj. 5, 6 (2) ; Mād-ch.
    12 ; W. **3**. 1, 2 ; Yt. **22**. 14 ;
    Yt. (Vtp.) 24. 60, 61.   Cf.
    frāyō°.

humata [*ča* W. Yt. **21**. 7, 9, 11,
    13, 15.

humataēšu [*ča* N. 84.

humatanąm A. 111 ; AG. 10 ;
    N. 22, 34, 46, 65 (2) ; Phl.
    Ys. **41**. 17 (Sp.) ; W. **3**. 2 ;
    Yt. (APZ.) 23. 8.

humatā [*čā* N. 28.

humatəm A. 25.

humate Yt. **22**. 15.

humaṭ T. 13 (read *a°*).

humananhaṭ T. 67.

humananhō Yt. 22. 18 ; Yt.
(Vtp.) 24. 17, 64.
humanō Yt. 22. 11, 12 ; Yt.
(Vtp.) 24. 58.
humanąm [*ča* Vij. p. 137.
humāīm N. 34.
humāyehe Vij. p. 151°; Yt.
(Vtp.) 24. 17.
humāyōtara N. 46.
humnəm W. 9. 2.
huraoδayå Yt. 22. 19.
huraoδahe Vij. p. 139; W. 5. 1.
huraoδəm W. 5. 2 ; Yt. (APZ.)
23. 6; Yt. (Vtp.) 24. 40.
huraoδō ZPGl. 6. 1.
huraōīm T. 97 (read ʿ*raoiδīm*).
hurąm N. 30.
huvaxšaṯ N. 46.
huvaxšāi N. 46.
huvačanhō Yt. (Vtp.) 24. 17.
huvirąm ZPGl. 5. 10.
husrava Yt. (APZ.) 23. 7 ; Yt·
(Vtp.) 24. 2.
huš N. 58.
hušiti Phl. Vd. 19. 2.
hušitōiš N. 47.
hušyaoθana Yt. 22. 11, 12.
hušyaoθanahe Yt. (Vtp.) 24·
17.
hušyaoθna Yt. (Vtp.) 24. 58.
hušyaoθnahe Yt. 22. 18.
hušyaōθnaṯ T. 67.
huš-hąm-sāstayāi Yt. 22. 18 ;
Yt. (Vtp.) 24. 64.
huzarštayå Yt. 22. 9 ; Yt.
(Vtp.) 24. 56.

huzvąm Yt. 22. 38.
hū N. 47, 48, 51, 58. Cf. *hū-frāšmō.*
hūxta T. 57 ; W. 3. 1, 2 ; Yt.
22. 14, 15 ; Yt. (Vtp.) 24.
60. Cf. *frāyō°.*
hūxtaēšu N. 84.
hūxta [*ča* W. Yt. 21. 7, 11.
hūxtanąm A. 111 ; N. 46 ; W.
3. 2.
hūxtā [*čā* N. 28.
hūxtəm A. 26.
hūxte Yt. (Vtp.) 24. 54, 61.
hū-frāšmō-dāiti Vij. p. 96.
hū-frāšmō-dāitīm N. 68.
hū-frāšmō-dātōiṯ N. 50.
hū-vaxšāṯ N. 48 (2).
hənta N. 52.
hənti N. 2, 33, 102 ; Phl. Vd.
1. 3, 14; 2. 41; 3. 40; 5.
19; 7. 52; v. l. T. 75 ; Vij.
p. 24; Yt. 22. 39; Yt. (Vtp.)
24. 18 (2), 51 (2).
həntū T. 75 (v. l. °*ti*).
həntəm Yt. (Vtp.) 24. 26.
hərəzaṯ cf. *fran°.*
hə̄ W. 8. 1.
hē A. 16 ; N. 3 (2), 6, 9 (2),
10 (2), 13, 16, 18, 20, 25,
27, 42 (3), 43, 45, 46, 79,
84, 101, 105 ; Phl. Vd. 7.
52 ; 18. 43 ; T. 80, 81, 92,
118 ; Vij. p. 23, 24 (2), 25
(2), 89, 126 (3), 127, 128,
138, 139, 145 (2), 146, 148 ;
Vth. 13 ; Yt. 22. 11, 18, 36 ;

Yt. (Vtp.) **24**. 9, 23, 31, 44, 47, 58, 64 (2). Cf. *paiti-šē.*
horā [ča ZPGl. 6. 3.
hō N. 42, 68; Phl. Vd. **2**. 5; **4**. 10; T. 110; W. Yt. **21**. 3 (6).
hōi N. 104; T. 101.
hā̊ A. 77, 78, 79, 80, 81.
haxšta cf. *a°.*
ham N. 11, 61, 62, 67, 97, 99 (4), 108; Phl. Vd. **7**. 52. Cf. *yāsaiti.*
hama Phl. Vd. **8**. 74.
haminō Phl. Vd. **1**. 3; **2**. 41.
hamō-nāfō Yt. (Vtp.) **24**. 9.
hampataiti Yt. (Vtp.) **24**. 26.
hampaθyeiti Yt. (Vtp.) **24**. 35.
ham-parštīm [ča Yt. (Vtp.) **24**. 60.
ham-parštəm [ča Yt. **22**. 14.
hambara Yt. (Vtp.) **24**. 39.
hamyāsaiti Phl. Vd. **7**. 52.
ham-sruṭ N. 24 (2).
htaštīm T. 97 (read *hutaš°*).
[hnəm] v. l. for *hunąm* Phl. Vd. **2**. 10, 18.
hya cf. *as°.*
hyaṭ N. 39, 42, 44, 109; W. **9**. 2.
hyāṭ N. 12; Yt. (Vtp.) **24**. 28.
hnm-šištō Yt. (Vtp.) **24**. 36 (read *ham°*).
hma N. 4.
hyātā N. 70.
hva N. 10; Phl. Vd. **2**. 5; Vij. p. 24; Yt. (Vtp.) **24**. 56.
hvaēibya N. 26.

hvaēibyō N. 26.
hvačaṇhaṭ T. 67.
hvačaṇhō Yt. **22**. 18; Yt. (Vtp.) **24**. 64.
hvačō Yt. **22**. 11, 12; Yt. (Vtp.) **24**. 58.
hvatō Phl. Vd. **12**. 4.
hvaθwarištō v. l. N. 11 (for *anvaθ°*).
hvaṭ Phl. Vd. **19**. 18.
hvarə Yt. (APZ.) **23**. 6; ZPGl. 13. 2.
hvarə-xšaētahe Vij. p. 186.
hvarə [ča Yt. (Vtp.) **24**. 43.
hvarəθanąm A. 16.
hvarəθəm cf. *pasuš°.*
hvarəšta T. 46. Cf. *frāyō.*
hvarəštaēšu [ča N. 84.
hvarəštanąm N. 46.
hvaršta Ganj. 5, 6 (2), 128; Mād-ch. 12; W. **3**. 1, 2; Yt. **22**. 14; Yt. (Vtp.) **24**. 60. Cf. *frāyō.*
hvaršta [ča W. Yt. **21**. 7, 11, 13, 15.
hvarštanąm W. **3**. 2.
hvarštayāi Yt. (Vtp.) **24**. 64.
hvaršte Yt. **22**. 15; Yt. (Vtp.) **24**. 54.
hvafna N. 15.
hvazāna Yt. (Vtp.) **24**. 48.
hvām Vth. 18.
hvāvōiš N. 55.
hvāvōya N. 55.
hvāzātō FD. 7.
hviš N. 58.

hvoištō ZPGl. 15. 5.
hvō N. 58; Phl. Vd. 7. 52;
  T. 112; Yt. (Vtp.) 24. 53.
hvōištō N. 1.

hvą̇θwō Yt. (APZ.) 23. 3.
hvą̇m Vij. p. 24, 180; ZPGl.
  32. 2.
hvą̇m[čiṭ T. 48 (2).

x᷿.

x᷿aine N. 26.
x᷿aētōuš Yt. (Vtp.) 24. 44.
x᷿aētvadaθahe Yt. (Vtp.) 24. 17.
x᷿aēδəm ZPGl. 11. 5.
x᷿aēpaiθe Yt. 22. 11; Yt.
  (Vtp.) 24. 58.
x᷿aēšu W. 4. 2.
x᷿atō Vij. p. 24.
x᷿aθrahe cf. aša°.
x᷿aδātahe Pars. p. 522; Yt.
  (Vtp.) 24. 24.
x᷿ap- cf. apanhabdənti.
x᷿afnanąm W Yt. 21. 5.
x᷿afnāδa W. Yt. 21. 11.
x᷿afrāδa W. Yt. 21. 13 (°nāδa?).
x᷿afrīrā Yt. (Vtp.) 24. 38.
x᷿afsata Yt. 22. 42 (3).
x᷿anha ZPGl. 5. 5.
x᷿aniraθəm W. Yt. 21. 14.
x᷿anəm N. 3.
x᷿anvå cf. asmō°.
x᷿araiti N. 30 (2).
x᷿arata N. 28, 46; Phl. Vd. 8.
  22.
x᷿araya N. 42.
x᷿arahe ZPGl. 36. 1.
x᷿arə Ep. M. 1. 4. 3.
x᷿arəitinąm W. Yt. 21. 5.
x᷿arə-xšaētahe Vij. p. 181.
x᷿arətōiṭ N. 29.

x᷿arəθa N. 55 (2), 64 (4); Yt.
  (Vtp.) 24. 45.
x᷿arəθanąm Yt. 22. 18, 36; Yt.
  (Vtp.) 24. 64.
x᷿arəθəm N. 28 (3); Phl. Ys. 3.
  21; Yt. 22. 18 (2), 36 (2),
  Yt. (Vtp.) 24. 64 (3).
x᷿arəθəma N. 66 (v. l. x᷿arəma).
x᷿arəθå Yt. (Vtp.) 24. 35. Cf.
  apaitiš°.
x᷿arənanha cf. paouru°.
x᷿arənanhatō N. 31, 46, 48, 58;
  Pars. p. 521, 532, 535 (2);
  Vij. p. 141, 164, (2); W.
  5. 1.
x᷿arənanhantəm Pars. p. 522;
  W. 5. 2.
x᷿arənanhuntəm Yt. (APZ.) 23.
  3.
x᷿arənanhe Yt. (Vtp.) 24. 38.
x᷿arənanhå Yt. (APZ.) 23. 1;
  Yt. (Vtp.) 24. 1.
x᷿arənas[ča Pars. p. 522 · Vij.
  p. 112; Yt. (Vtp.) 24. 34, 46.
x᷿arənazdå Yt. (Vtp.) 24. 38.
x᷿arənō N. 30; Phl. Vd. 5. 9
  (2). Yt. (Vtp.) 24. 8, 40, 46.
x᷿arənå cf. duš°.
x᷿arənta N. 52.
x᷿arənti cf. aiwi°.

x^varəntīš Yt. (Vtp.) **24**. 36.

x^varəm N. 45.

x^varəma N. 67.

x^varō N. 30 (2).

x^varōiṯ N. 45.

x^varō-čiθrəm ZPGl. 7. 8.

x^varštəm. A. 27.

x^vasurō ZPGl. 5. 7.

x^vastarahe Vij. p. 127.

x^vastāitīm N. 47 ; W. **5**. 2.

x^vastātayå W. **5**. 1.

x^vāsty[*å*] N. 47.

x^vāiš FD. 7 ; Phl. Vd. **4**. 1.

x^vāθra T. 83.   Cf. *pouru°* and *vīspō°.*

x^vāθrəm[*ča* N. 47.

x^vāθrō-nahīm Yt. (Vtp.) **24**. 6.

x^vādaēnå T. 77.

x^vāparąm CB.

x^vāstāitīm N. 47.

x^vāstāiš[*ča* N. 57 (3).

x^vāstrahe N. 47 ; Yt. (APZ.) **23**. 7.

x^vāhva T. 107.

x^vistō N. 108.

x^vtəm[*čiṯ* ZPGl. 8. 8 (R. *ant°*).

x^vyāθa Yt. (Vtp.) **24**. 12.

x^vyāṯ Yt. (Vtp.) **24**. 42.